LOST COUNTRY HOUSES OF NOTTINGHAMSHIRE

MAXWELL CRAVEN

AMBERLEY

For my kinsman Richard Craven-Smith-Milnes, without whom Winkburn Hall would have become another lost house.

This edition first published 2025

Amberley Publishing
The Hill, Stroud
Gloucestershire GL5 4EP

www.amberley-books.com

British Library Cataloguing in Publication Data.
A catalogue record for this book is available from the British Library.

ISBN 978 1 3981 1833 1 (print)
ISBN 978 1 3981 1834 8 (ebook)

Typeset by Simon and Sons ITES Services Pvt. Ltd., Chennai, India.
Printed in Great Britain.

Appointed GPSR EU Representative: Easy Access System Europe Oü, 16879218
Address: Mustamäe tee 50, 10621, Tallinn, Estonia
Contact Details: gpsr.requests@easproject.com, +358 40 500 3575

Contents

Introduction

Sir Roy Strong, in his introduction to 'The Destruction of the Country House' exhibition held at the Victoria and Albert Museum (V&A) in 1974, wrote of the way that, in the British countryside, we then took for granted our country houses. 'Like our parish churches,' he wrote, 'the country houses seem always to have been there, since time immemorial part of the fabric of our heritage.' It would seem invidious to add that in 1974 we also took for granted the vicarage, the pub, the shop, the post office and the pleasure of sharing a stirrup cup with the meet on Boxing Day – all institutions and, if anything, even more under threat today than the country house.

Throughout the twentieth century and into the twenty-first, we have suffered an alarming loss of such buildings, their settings, contents and the way of life they supported. Their destruction represents one of the greatest losses of our art history – architecture, craftsmanship, fine art, furniture, sculpture, archives, all. The 1974 V&A exhibition had sufficient impact to have changed all that, and the tide of destruction was gradually rolled back. From 1979, this was aided by the progressive diminution of the personal tax burden (a trend regrettably reversed in the present century), which once more began to make the possibility of living in a large house in the country a viable proposition. This, in turn, led to a renewed interest in traditional trades and provided a wider choice of employment in the countryside.

In Nottinghamshire, in the years since 1969, when listed building consent was first required prior to the demolition of the listed building (previously only notification to RCHM was required), only five substantial houses have been lost, but even then, one – Blyth – was already a ruined shell, despite being by far the most important of the group. Yet in the years from 1945 to 1968, no fewer than twenty-four were destroyed, including important buildings like Grove, Rufford, Ossington, Watnall, Kirkby Old Hall and Thorney. Before that, the destruction was even worse. The figures speak for themselves. Nottinghamshire's worst year – its *annus horribilis* – was actually 1964, when four houses fell to the contractor's ball and chain; thereafter, destruction was more evenly spread. Yet even a decade before the listing of buildings was mooted, 1937 saw three casualties. The 1968 Town and Country Planning Act and the 1974 exhibition together were thus a watershed, and these figures repeat for most lowland counties.

Yet for all this, country houses have been destroyed right through the last millennium for a wide variety of reasons; there have always been losses, as this book shows. The most common reason for the destruction of an important house before 1919 – apart from the random but ever-present threat of fire – was usually the desire of the owner to improve the standard of his accommodation, or to expand it, often commensurate with a rise in status. In the nineteenth century, an agricultural boom, which lasted throughout the middle years until around 1873, coupled with a superfluity of labour, caused households to expand, and more and better standards of service accommodation were required. Some owners met these needs by enlarging, others by demolition and replacement. Other factors include the amalgamation of estates, war (especially the English Civil War), plague, urban expansion, trunk road widening, mining, lack of tenants, land requisition for infrastructure, financial pressure and taxation (Lloyd George's death duties especially), local authority neglect, philistinism and sheer bloody-mindedness. Of these, housing developments and the expansion of coal mines have been far and away the most persistent cause of destruction.

The demolition of houses, therefore, can be seen as a continuing process of loss and renewal until the last century, when a host of new factors came into play: losses accelerated alarmingly and little in terms of renewal was on offer. It is this last factor that, until the 1980s, was most worrying, as a substantial and largely unsung portion of our cultural and artistic heritage was swept away in a holocaust of destruction over some sixty-five years, 1919–74, when thirty-eight out of the county total of houses were destroyed.

This book aims to give a brief written summary and visual record of the majority of the losses, as far as the available images permit, with brief descriptive and historical captions, and may be viewed as a locally complementary work to add fine detail to Giles Worsley's *The Lost Houses of Britain* (Aurum Press/Country Life, 2002) and an amplification and variation of Philip Jones' excellent book on lost Nottinghamshire houses (2006). I have concentrated on country houses – all high-status dwellings in some degree – for they are best documented; lost town houses and what estate agents like to call 'village houses' have been mainly eschewed as one could fill another book with the losses from Nottingham alone. One or two houses embedded in towns have survived my cull, however, like Chauntry House at Newark or Gilcroft House at Mansfield, which one might class as quasi-country houses. There is hardly space to devote to the parks, gardens and art treasures affected by these losses, too, but much more detailed information can often be found in the indispensable pages of the Transactions of the Thoroton Society.

Nottinghamshire is, of course, famous as being home to the Dukeries, but the great ducal houses have not fared well. Most of the great ducal families got involved in mining, either by leasing out the land and taking a cut or by forming mining concerns themselves; indeed, it explains the sheer scale of some of their seats. People also tend to ask which dukes had stakes in Nottinghamshire, for people usually just think of Newcastle (Haughton, Clumber, Welbeck, Kirkby Hardwick and Broxtowe) and Portland (Welbeck, Bulwell Wood). Nevertheless, apart from those two (of which Newcastle represents four different creations and has still managed to become extinct), there were those of Kingston (Thoresby, Sneinton, etc.), St Albans (Bestwood), briefly, in Queen Anne's reign, Shrewsbury (Worksop, Rufford, Stoke Bardolph), Norfolk (Worksop) and Rutland (Greasley, Averham and Kelham), not to mention bordering dukes, like Devonshire, with holdings in the county.

The following entries are by date of demolition (occasionally approximate), rather than cause of loss or date of building and where the house was listed by what is now Historic England, that is included in the heading, and I have added 'SAM' for a Scheduled Ancient Monument. If remains are listed, they are included.

Section One

Losses Before 1700

1. Laxton Castle (SAM), after 1340

While Laxton is most famed for the durability of its open field system, it is also notable for its castle, probably the largest in area in the county, the remains of which (a substantial motte and two baileys) are clearly visible to the north of the village and reached by a field road and footpath opposite the parish church. The outer bailey (also see Laxton Manor) is particularly spacious, emphasising the plateau-like nature of the site, and the dividing balk between it and the inner bailey with its topping of bocage neatly terminates the view from the site's entrance. Beyond, the still deeply moated motte rises to give commanding views, especially to the east and north. The castle, undoubtedly residential as well as defensive, was built in stone by Robert de Cauz, son-in-law of Domesday grandee Geoffrey Alselin, who had put up a timber motte-and-bailey fortification there in the late eleventh century. It came to the Everinghams through the Birkin family in 1230, Adam de Everingham (1st Lord Everingham from 1309) entertained Edward I

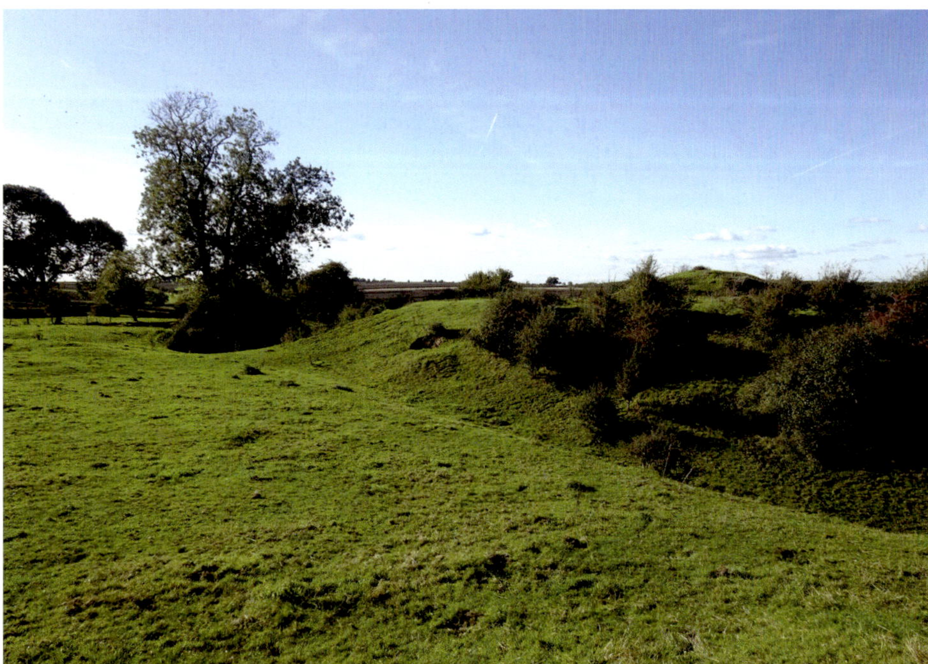

The site of Laxton Castle, showing the motte and part of the inner bailey, looking north-west, October 2023. (M. Craven)

and the dying Queen Eleanor in the castle for five days in November 1290. The castle itself was only abandoned (and gradually dismantled for the stone by the locals) after the death of the last Everingham, Robert, in 1387, the Ettons, their heirs having their chief seat elsewhere. It was replaced by a Tudor manor house (see p. 14).

2. Clipstone Lodge (SAM and II), *c.* 1525

What remains are the core of what were once ashlar walls of white Mansfield stone. They include a Romanesque arched recess and are the vestiges of a royal hunting lodge and later administrative centre, built, it is now thought, in the early years of the reign of Henry II (1154–89) and probably replicates the semi-fortified site at Kingshaugh, Darlton, where the present farmhouse contains elements of a similar lodge. It boasted a gatehouse, a great hall, several substantial chambers and a domestic chapel. It was visited by most of the kings between then and the end of the fourteenth century, and although no record survives of a fifteenth-century royal visit, two campaigns of restoration were undertaken before Edward IV granted it to George, Duke of Clarence. It was in 'great dekay & ruyne' by 1525 and was robbed for its stone. From the eighteenth century it has also been known as King John's Palace. It was excavated on *Time Team* in 2011.

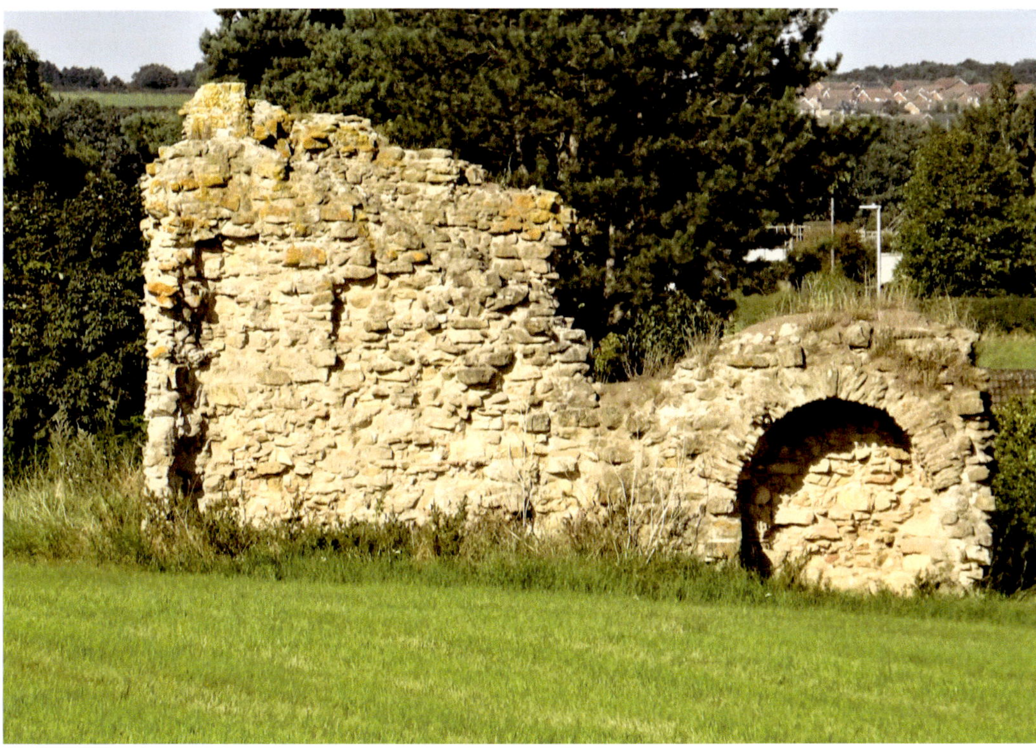

Part of the standing remains of Clipstone Palace, looking east, September 2023. (M. Craven)

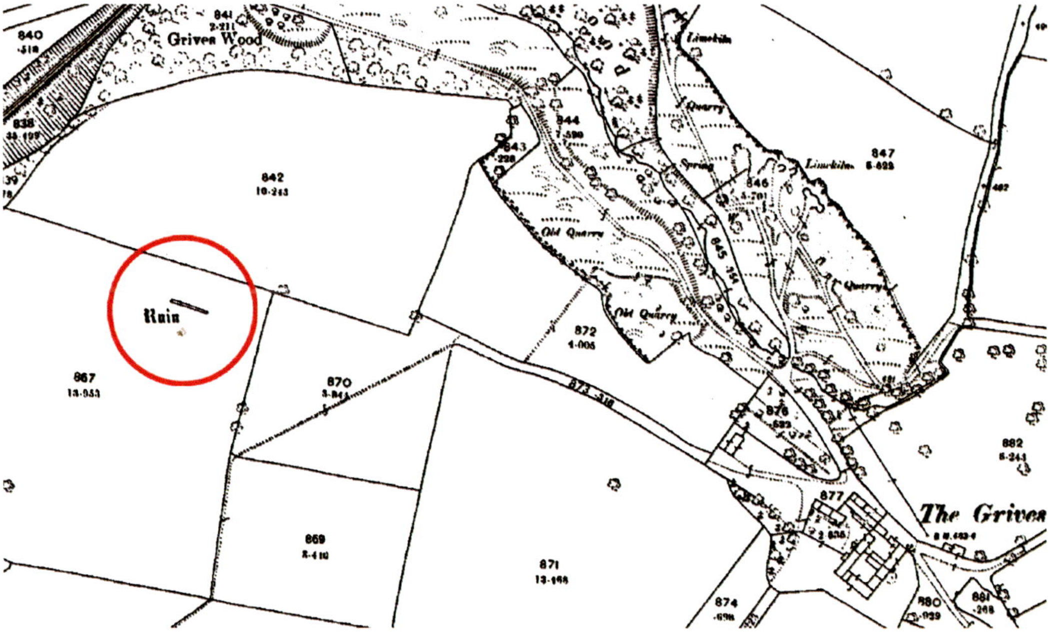

Kirkby, marked as 'ruin' on the 1:2,500 Ordnance map of 1879/81. (National Library of Scotland)

3. Kirk(e)by (SAM), 1599

Sir Charles Cavendish, third son of Bess of Hardwick, decided to build himself a new brick and stone seat at Kirkby on Grives Hill, opposite the (long-lost) castle in 1597, and work began to a design by Robert Smythson soon afterwards. Sir Charles had acquired the estate, called Kirkby Hardwick (see p. 82), from the Conyers family, who had inherited it from the d'Arcys of Knaith. However, a feud with Sir John Stanhope of Shelford led to a sanguinary confrontation in 1599 while Cavendish was present inspecting the works, causing him to abandon the project in favour of Welbeck. Smythson's drawings of a considerable house, of 'hour glass' plan and ground-floor colonnades, were identified by the late Mark Girouard from the plan as revealed by crop marks seen in 1963 and 1976. The stone was subsequently requisitioned by Cavendish and his architect for the building of Bolsover Castle, but the standing remains noted on the 1877 25-inch OS map were cleared in 1971.

4. Wollaton Old Hall (II), by 1620

The original capital mansion at Wollaton was probably built by the medieval lords there, the Morteynes, although no account of it survives. However, the place came into the possession of the Willoughby family (from Willoughby on the Wolds, originally called Bugge) in 1312, but they did not live there until about 1462, by which time the Morteyne's house may well have been long abandoned. At this time the house lay north of the present Admiral Rodney inn in the village, enlarged in the late fifteenth century, the Willoughbys' wealth being supercharged

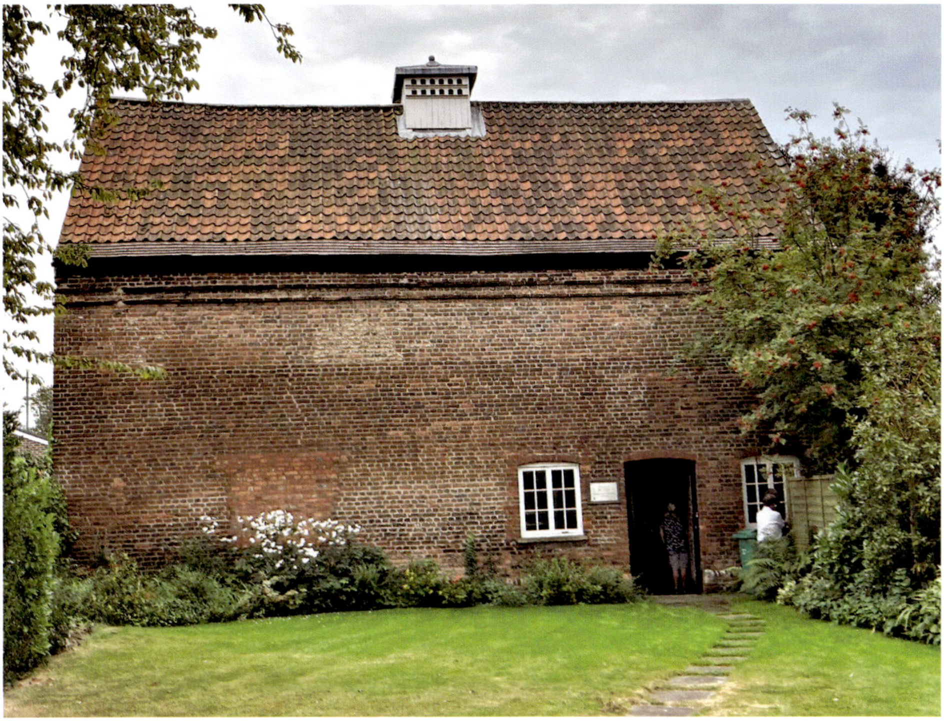

Wollaton Hall's surviving brick dovecote, seen restored in September 2023. (M. Craven)

by burgeoning coal mining interests. This house was essentially abandoned too once Sir Francis Willoughby had moved into the present mansion, and it is recorded as ruinous in the 1620s. In around 1567/68, Sir Francis added a dovecote to the old hall, in brick with a surviving pantile roof and low glover or cupola with an original arched S entrance under a hood mould, flanked by Willoughby's initials in blue brick. This survived and was converted into stables in the 1880s, but following the sale of the estate in 1926, it rapidly became derelict, only being restored through dedicated local efforts in the 1960s. It is now an excellent locally run museum in Dovecote Drive (where else?) and open two Sundays per month.

5. Scrooby Manor (II), 1637

The earliest reference to the medieval manor house or Palace of the Archbishops of York occurs in 1207 when King John ordered French wine to be sent to Scrooby for the use of his half-brother, who was the archbishop at that time – the house seems to have been a sort of halfway stopping-off point for archbishops journeying from York to London. It was 'a great manor place standinge withyn a mote' according to Leland, set round two courtyards and timber framed but with 'the front of the hall' in brick. In 1558 the gatehouse and some other parts were demolished and further work done in brick. In 1530 Cardinal Wolsey spent the September there when he fell out of favour with King Henry VIII,

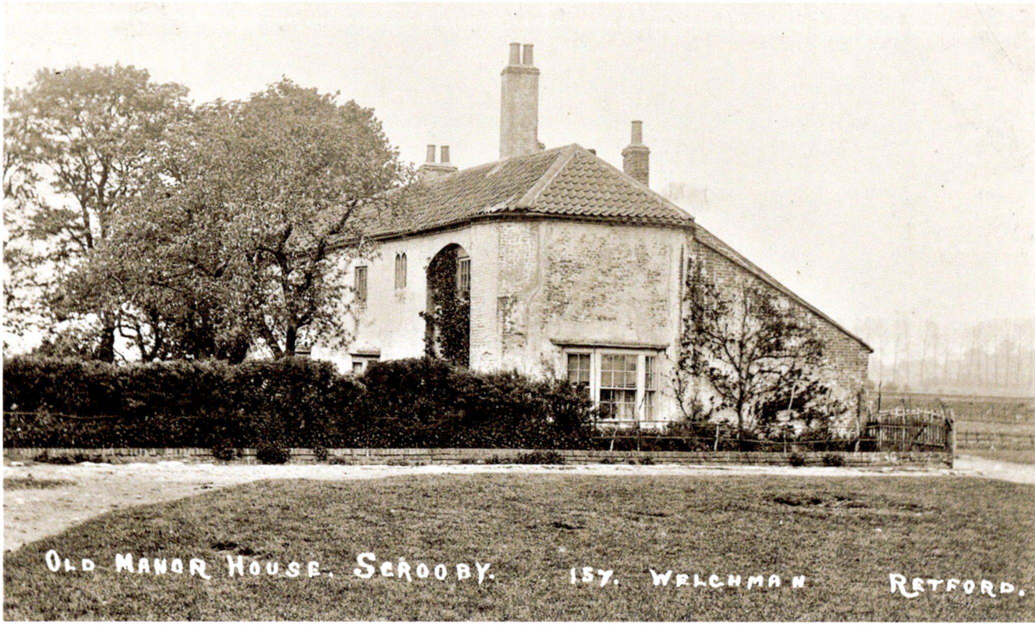

The surviving portion of the former manor house at Scrooby, adapted as a farmhouse and photographed before 1905. From a postcard. (James Darwin)

who himself apparently stayed there in 1541. William Brewster, the famous religious separatist who in 1620 travelled to America on the *Mayflower*, was born there, son of the archbishop's bailiff. The house was partly demolished in 1637, but in the mid-eighteenth century that part of it not robbed away by local people to rebuild their own homes was converted into a farmhouse, leaving a couple of two light mullioned medieval windows and a two-storey blind recessed arch. It has been recently restored by its owners after being for many years divided as cottages.

6. Hawton Manor (SAM), by 1642

Hawton passed from the Comptons to the Molyneux family of Teversal. The former, probably in the person of Sir Robert de Compton, had built a house within a moat there around a courtyard, likely in the early fourteenth century and doubtless from his knightly status. The estate came in the late fifteenth century to Sir Thomas Molyneux, who was there in 1482 and 1487. His son, Sir Edward, a prominent judge, moved his residence to nearby Thorpe. By the time that the family had sold the estate to the Newdigates, the timber-framed house was probably long in decay. Indeed, the house platform and moat, protected by the River Devon on two sides, was converted into a redoubt, with artillery stationed there during the Civil War and the site is still known as the Hawton Redoubt.

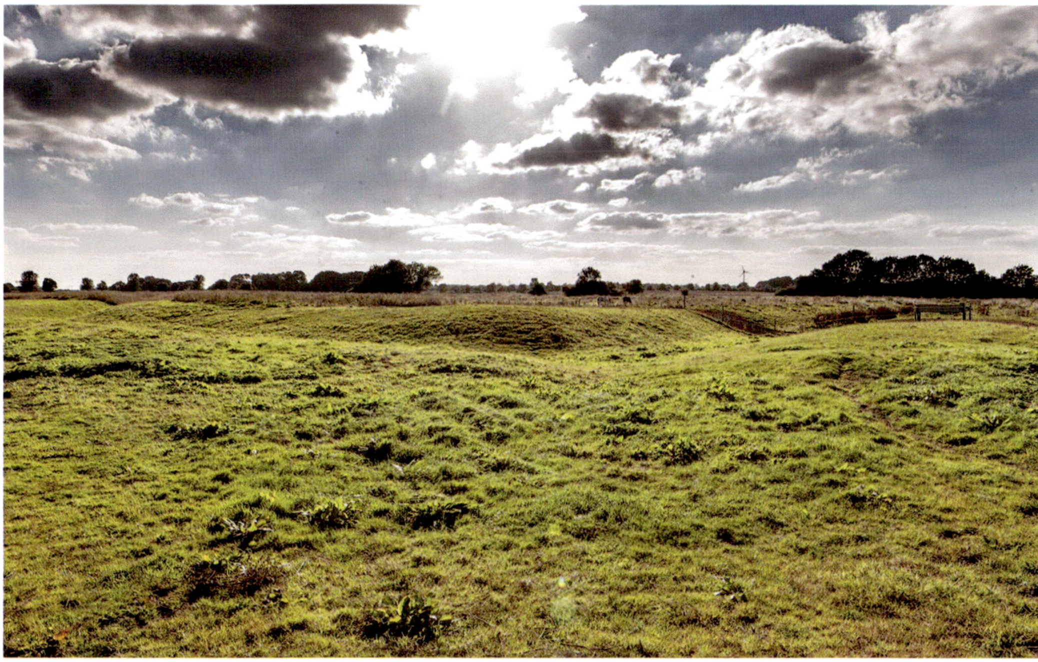

Site of the manor house at Hawton, looking south-west. Photographed in 2012. (Private collection)

7. Wiverton Hall (II*), 1645

The house, originally moated with a domestic chapel, was replaced on part of his ancestral estates by Sir Thomas Chaworth *c.* 1450, but underwent a fairly thorough rebuilding in 1615–16 for Sir George Chaworth (later MP) to designs by John Smythson. Sir George was, in 1627, created 1st Viscount Chaworth in the Irish Peerage so he could be honoured while retaining his Parliamentary seat, but he died in 1639, being succeeded by his son John. John was a keen Royalist once the Civil War had broken out and, in December 1642, began to fortify the house which he garrisoned for the king for almost three years with 400 men, despite a deteriorating military situation. In June 1643, Queen Henrietta, on her way from Newark, wrote to the king: 'I shall sleep at Werton [Wiverton], and thence to Ashby, where we will resolve what way to take.' Lord Chaworth was obliged to surrender, after a lengthy siege, to the Parliamentary commander Sydenham Poyntz, after which the severely damaged house was almost entirely destroyed, leaving only the gatehouse. The latter, despite its four-centered arch, shows clear signs of the hand of Smythson, with a typically wide sixteen-light mullion and transom window on each floor above and nail head parapet. This survived as a farmhouse, but after the estate had passed via an heiress to John Musters it was incorporated into a new house in 1814, which eventually left the family in 1938.

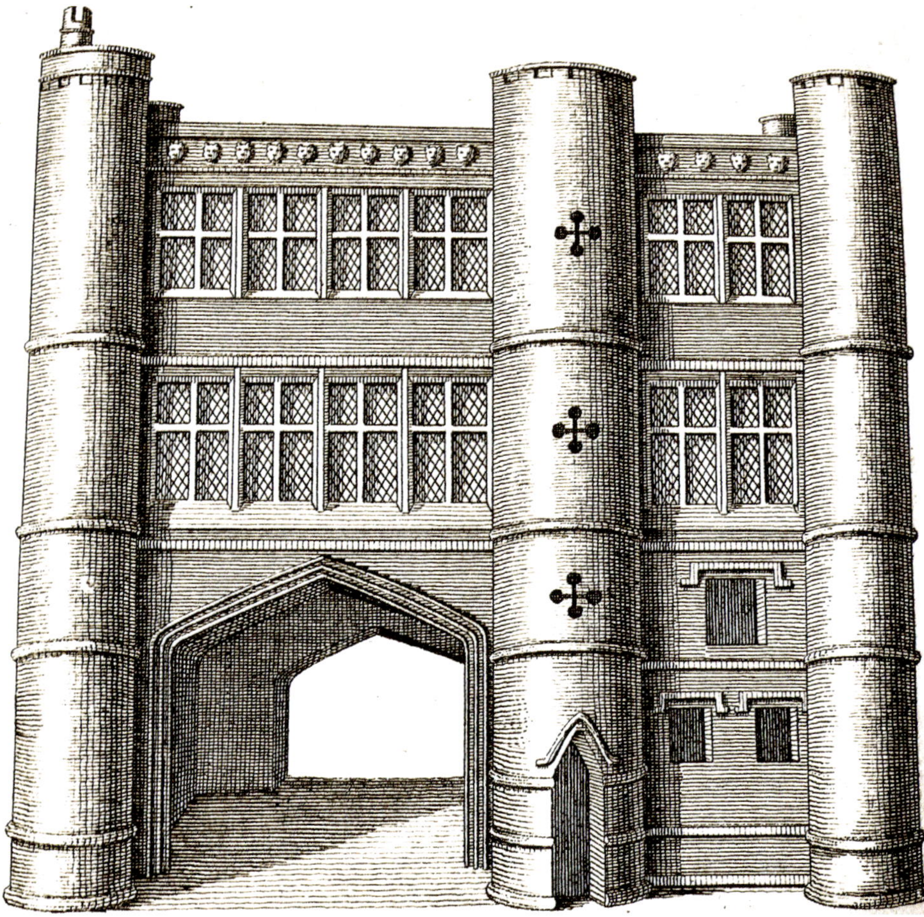

The gatehouse from the old manor house at Wiverton, as incorporated in the present house, from Throsby. (M. Craven)

8. Newark Castle (I and SAM), 1648

The site was granted to the bishops of Lincoln by Henry I to make 'a ditch and rampart'. By 1139 a castle had been established which was soon expanded in stone. The finished building was notable for having been the site of the death of King John on 18 October 1216 and it had also served as a mint until 1154. It was much rebuilt in the 1320s, and Donald, Earl of Mar, added the towers on the river front shortly afterwards. The castle passed to the Crown in 1538 and was held on lease by Sir Francis Leake of Sutton Scarsdale and then by Lord Burghley, who re-fortified it. It was the centre of the siege of Newark – the third of three – from November 1645 until May 1646 when it again served as a (makeshift) mint for the king. It was slighted in 1648 and mouldered quietly away until 1845, when it was consolidated by the architect Anthony Salvin, being handed over to the Corporation of Newark in time for Queen Victoria's golden jubilee celebrations.

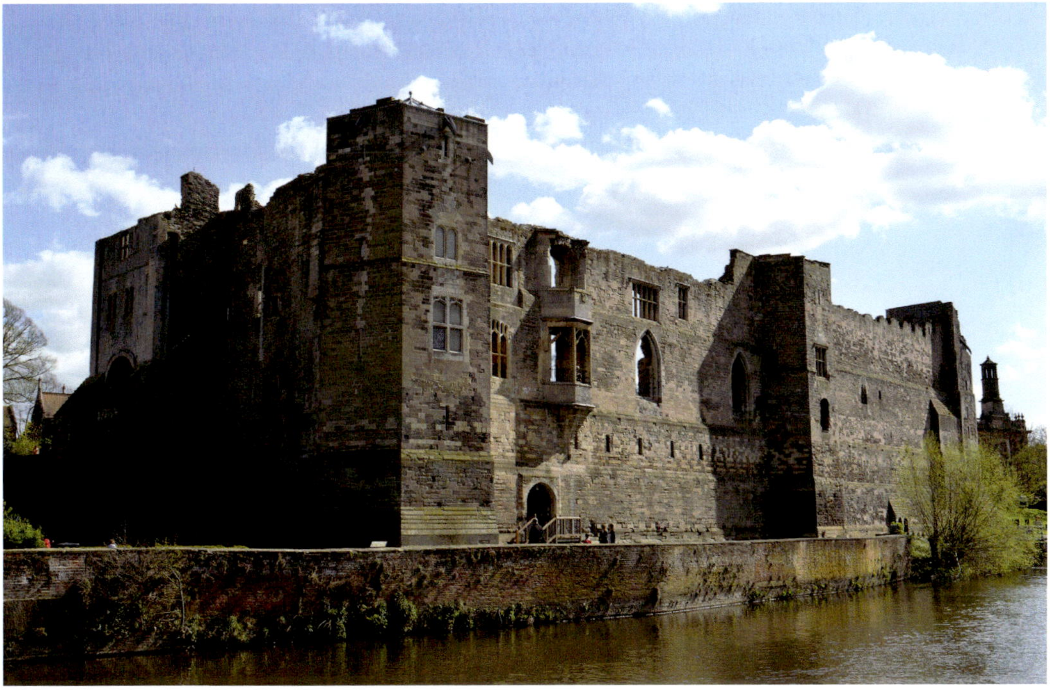

Newark Castle photographed looking south-east from Riverside Park, 2017. (C. Craven)

9. Manor, Stoke Bardolph, by 1650

A house shown on a map in the National Archives of 1592, against which is written 'The Erl of Shrewsbury Stoke Bardolfe', would appear from its plan and elevation to have been relatively newly built. It was a two-storey building with attic gables and a five-bay centre with cross-wings beyond, reminiscent of

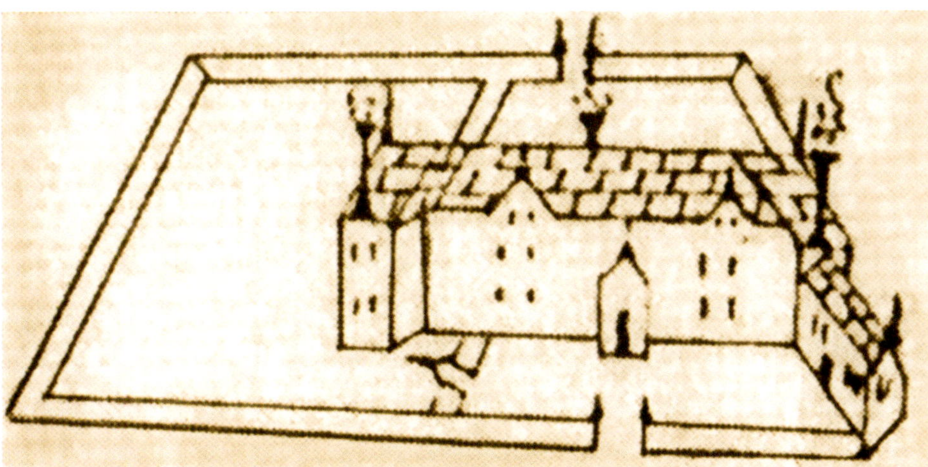

Stoke Bardolph Hall, from an old survey. (PRO)

Robert Smythson's plan for Kirkby. There is a gabled porch and a service range to one side – suggesting that the surviving view may be of the north side – surrounded by wall. The manorial estate appears to have been divided after the attainder of Viscount Lovell, whose timber-framed manor house (inherited from the Bardolphs) stood opposite. Later, after being acquired by Sir Thomas Stanhope of Shelford, it came into the hands of the 6th Earl of Shrewsbury, who clearly decided to build anew on a fresh site. Conceivably this house could be an unrecorded design by Robert Smythson, but if so it would date from the time he was building Wollaton. That it failed to survive the seventeenth century is all that is known of its fate.

10. Laxton Manor (SAM), after 1660

After the two-generation tenure of the Etton family, part of Laxton came to John Roose in 1435 and he set about buying up as much as possible of other elements that had become detached. At first, the family did not live at Laxton, but after the death of Humphrey Roos in 1531 his son built a new manor house, presumably using much of the stone still available on-site, of which neither picture nor description exists. It stood in the outer bailey facing east–west, hard against

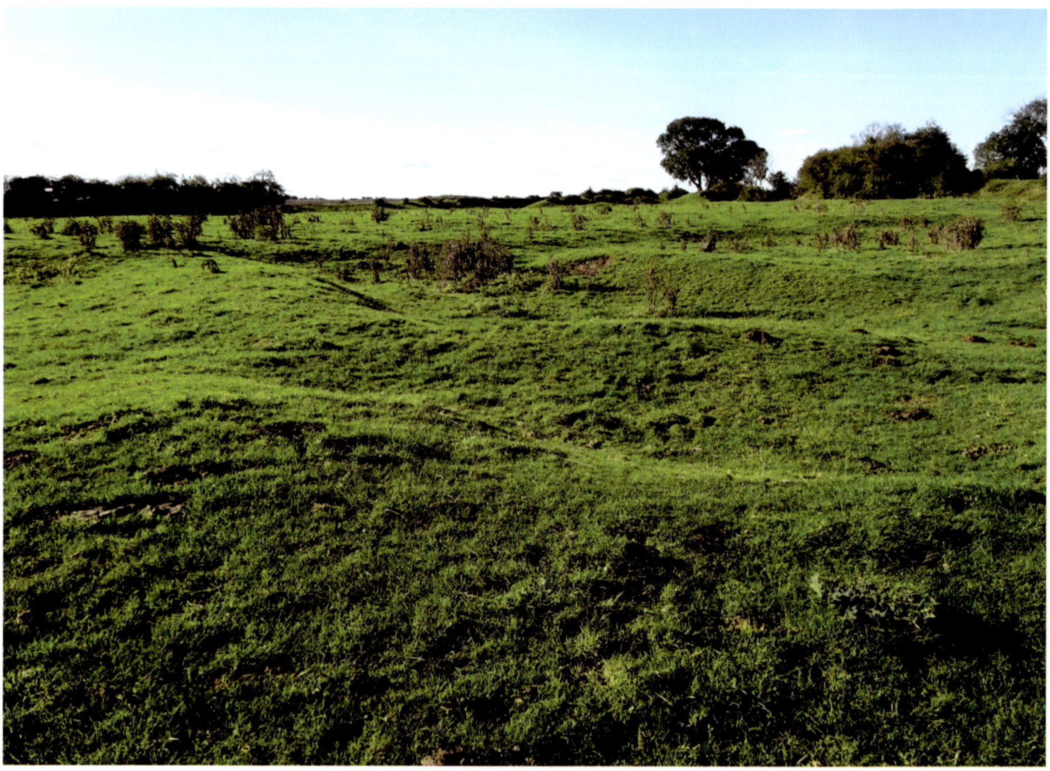

Laxton Manor House site, looking north-west, October 2023. (Carole Craven)

the division with the inner bailey. Humphrey's son Peter was beggared by the profligacy of his second wife and his own misfortunes and died in 1605, leaving the estate heavily encumbered. In consequence, his son sold everything left for £6,000 to the Marquess (later Duke) of Buckingham, dying without issue shortly afterwards. However, the family were very prolific and male descendants (called Ross and Rose) were living in humble circumstances locally into the early twentieth century. Buckingham sold the estate to a Flemish *arriviste* called Sir William Courten, whose son sold it again in 1640 to Robert Pierrepont, 1st Earl of Kingston. The house, not lived in since Buckingham had bought it (and by then quite probably in a state of decay), was demolished once Kingston had recovered from his support of the king after the Restoration. The last Earl Manvers, the Pierreponts' heir, sold the estate to the Crown in 1952.

11. Greasley Castle (II and SAM), after 1677

Originally a motte-and-bailey castle of the twelfth century, Greasley was built by William, son of Hugh de Greasley. The heiress brought the property to Nicholas de Cantilupe of Ilkeston on the other side of the Erewash, who obtained a licence to crenellate his house in 1330, which included at least two drum angle towers, and he also emparked it. House and estate passed to the Zouches of Codnor Castle, who already had a similar house across the river nearby, and its decay almost certainly began at this point. In the Wars of the Roses, it became Crown

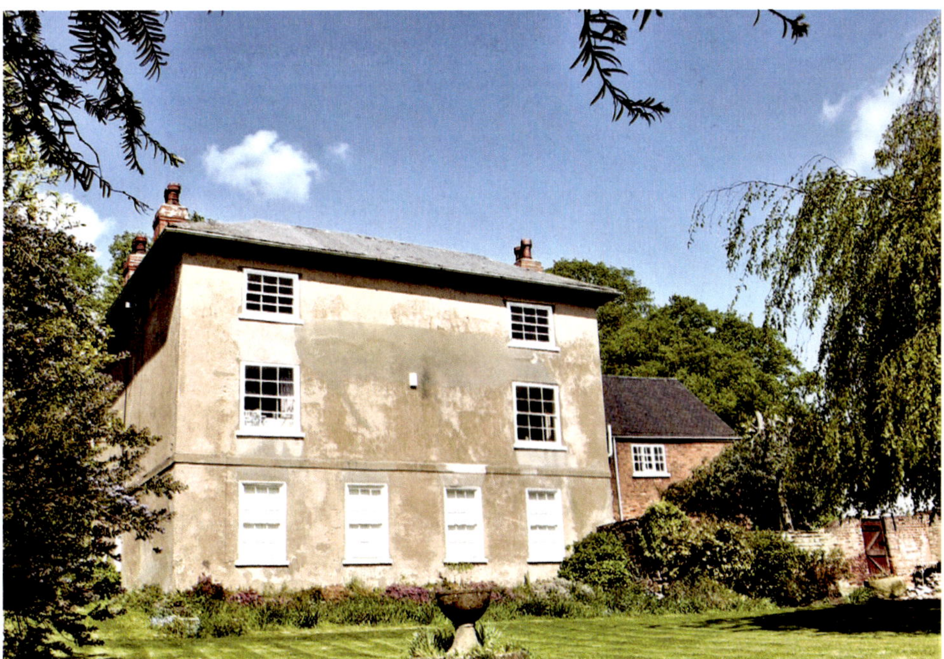

Greasley Castle with a Regency farmhouse occupying part of the site. (Berry & Co.)

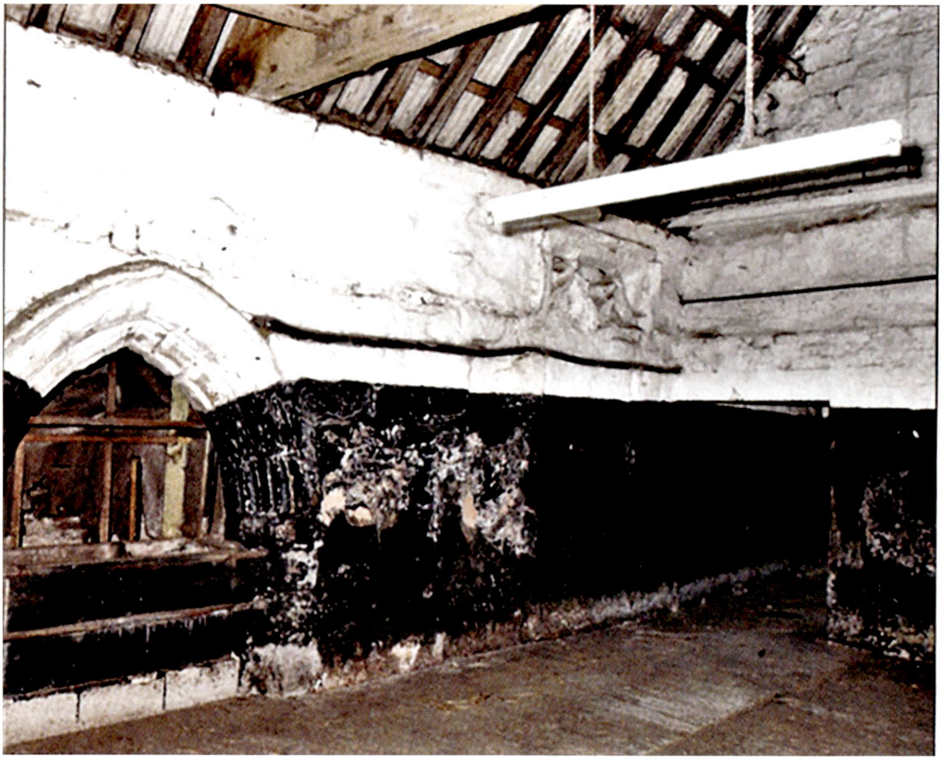

Surviving upper part of a Gothic window incorporated into an eighteenth-century barn. (Berry & Co.)

property until Henry VII granted it to Sir John Savage, whose posterity sold it to the Manners, earls (later dukes) of Rutland in 1677, who let it as a farm. Redundant for over a century, it was gradually dismantled, Throsby noting that in 1796 it was 'totally destroyed except a plain old wall or two'. Portions still to be seen are a barn and other outbuildings of the large stuccoed Regency villa (the farmhouse), built by the Barbers of Lamb Close on part of the site and including some vestiges of the original fortified manor house.

Section Two

Losses 1700–99

12. Rampton Manor (I), 1726

The manorial estate descended from Robert de Rampton, who held it in 1086 from Roger de Busli via an heiress to Robert de Maulovel, from whose descendants it passed in 1374 to John Stanhope MP. By 1552 it had come via a Stanhope heiress to John Babington (d. 1563), who appears to have rebuilt the house in high Tudor style. A map from a later era shows that it had an east–west great hall range of two storeys with a central entrance enclosed on either side by lodgings. Those of the east side consisted of a cross-wing with family accommodation under a hipped roof and service accommodation to the north. The Babington heiress Sanchia married Derbyshire grandee Sir Gervase Eyre in 1607, whose descendant Anthony Eyre MP demolished the old house in 1726. The only standing relic is an ornamental ashlar gateway on the edge of the churchyard, consisting of a depressed and enriched ogiform arch with a panel of arms above. It is flanked by two smaller panels with a niche above, all framed by a well-moulded cranked parapet, presumably echoing the detailing likely to have embellished the lost mansion itself. A considerable stretch of original brick-and-ashlar-dressed walling still forms the east boundary of the churchyard (see also Rampton Manor, p. 55)

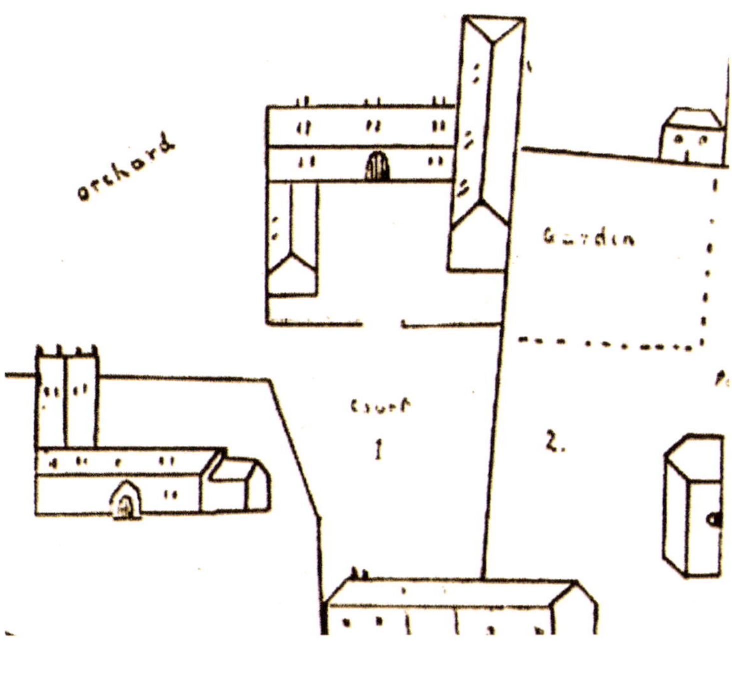

Rampton Manor House as depicted on a survey of 1717. (Thoroton Society)

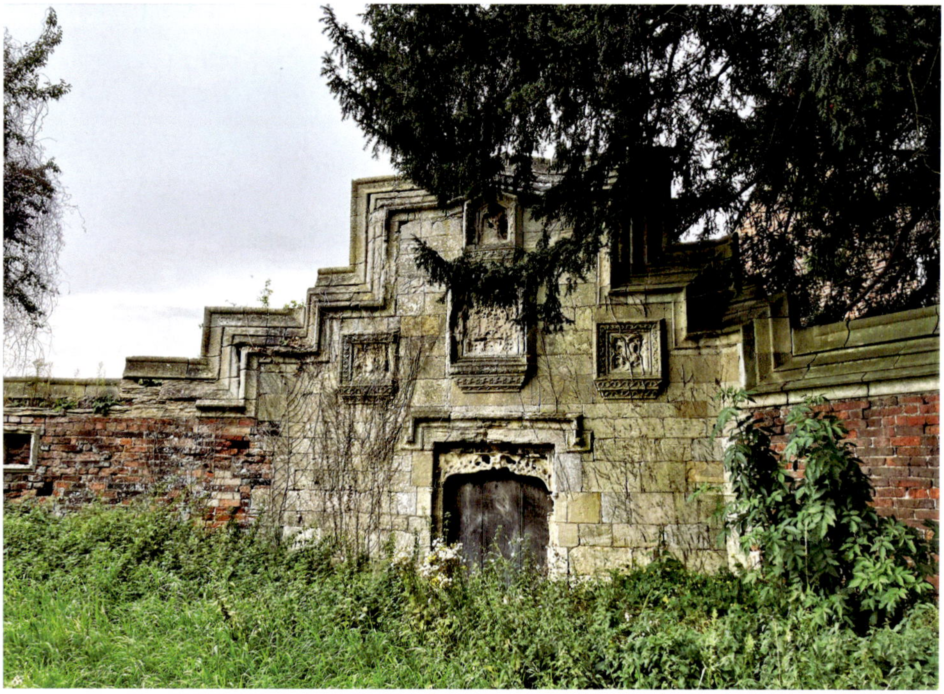

Surviving and richly decorated fragment of the gatehouse of Rampton Manor in the churchyard, September 2023. (Carole Craven)

13. Ossington (Old) Hall, 1728

The estate at Ossington was given by its tenant-in-chief, Ralph de Burun, to the Knights of St John of Jerusalem, who after litigation with the Cistercians over their endowment retained it until the Dissolution of the Monasteries. It was then, after being held and reduced by some intermediaries, acquired by Gregory Cartwright, who died in 1574, leaving his son George (d. 1612) to build a new family house. Of stone, it was of two storeys with attics, the main front (as illustrated in Thoroton) consisting of three bays, each crowned by a crow-stepped gable and a ball finial, and interrupted by a chimney breast carrying a trio of plainish chimneys. The rooms were lit by six-light mullion and transom windows, although from the lack of one on the first floor at bay one there is a suggestion of a Smythson-style meandering staircase rising towards the attics. To the left was a single-storey brick extension, presumably mid-seventeenth century, and there was another wing at the right-hand end of the façade, made rather too narrow in the drawing. Beyond that was a parterre garden and outbuildings beyond. Assuming the drawing shows the south front, the entrance was probably in the east. Here, the Cartwrights lived quite happily until 1726, when George Cartwright decided to build a more modern and more spacious house and, when it was completed, the old house was duly swept away (see also Ossington Hall, pp. 71–72).

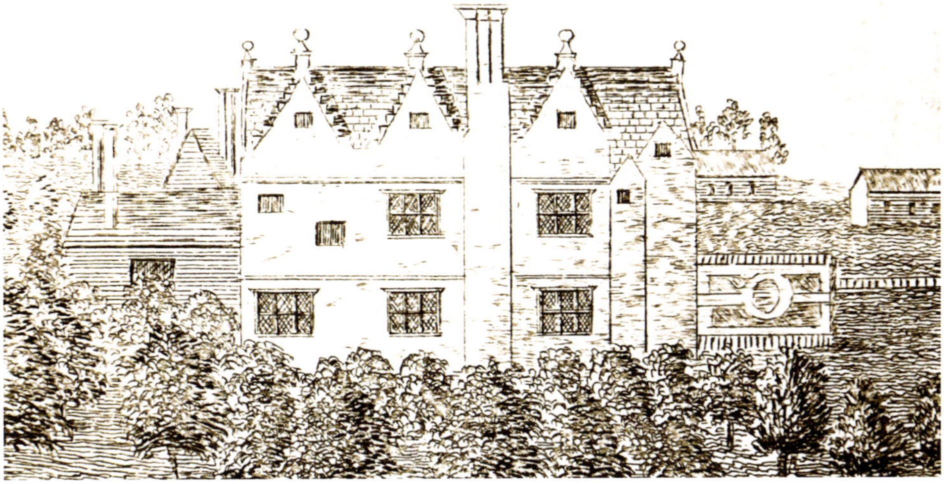

Ossington Old Hall, south front, 1676. From a print. (Private collection)

14. Sibthorpe Hall (SAM), *c.* 1740

Anciently the estate of the Sibthorpes, where Thomas de Sibthorpe later founded a monastic institution. From them it passed in 1394 to the Leekes, who held it on behalf of the Knights Hospitallers until the Dissolution of the Monasteries when, in 1545, it was granted to Richard Whalley, who built a large new house and created a park. According to a note in the Portland MSS, the house was in 1608 called Chantry House or College House. A dovecote is also mentioned, which was the only material survivor of the house when Throsby wrote in 1791, as the rest seems to have been abandoned and largely demolished by the

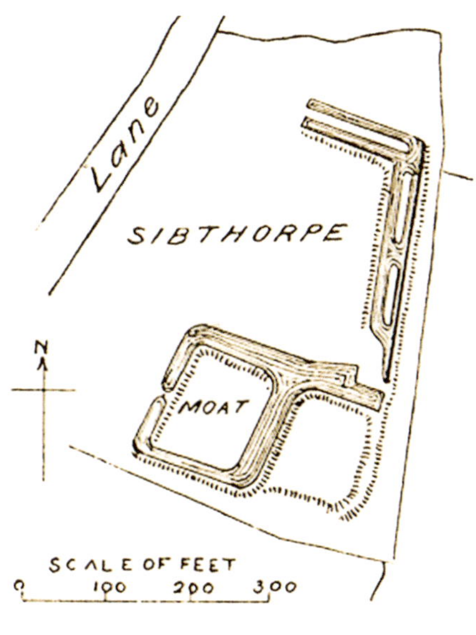

Plan of the moated site at Sibthorpe, from the Nottinghamshire *Victoria County History*. (M. Craven)

mid-eighteenth century. William Senior's map of 1629 shows an L-shaped range of buildings with more buildings to the north-west. This general arrangement has been more recently confirmed by archaeological surveying. Rooms and partition walls were identified, in addition to the main exterior walls. Extending to the north-west and south-west, further foundations were identified, which were perhaps the kitchens and other service areas. To the west were a series of less well-defined anomalies, interpreted as outbuildings, workshops or stables. To the south were curvilinear high-resistance anomalies, thought to be embankments, forming landscaping features around a garden.

15. Thoresby, 1746

Robert Pierrepont of Holme, created 1st Earl of Kingston (-upon-Hull) in 1628, acquired the estate at Thoresby in 1633, but had little time to develop it before the outbreak of the Civil War in 1642. Like Lord Chaworth at Wiverton (see p. 11), he was a keen Royalist, but rather than losing his house he instead had the misfortune to lose his life in action in 1643. It was left to his son, Henry, raised to the Marquessate of Dorchester (on Thames), to build a house, for which the design survives, drawn by Colen Campbell almost certainly after one by William Talman, in Vol. I of *Vitruvius Britannicus*. With mason Banjamin Jackson (who worked with Talman at Chatsworth), he produced a French baroque three-storey thirteen-bay house of immense distinction the main front set off by a two-storey,

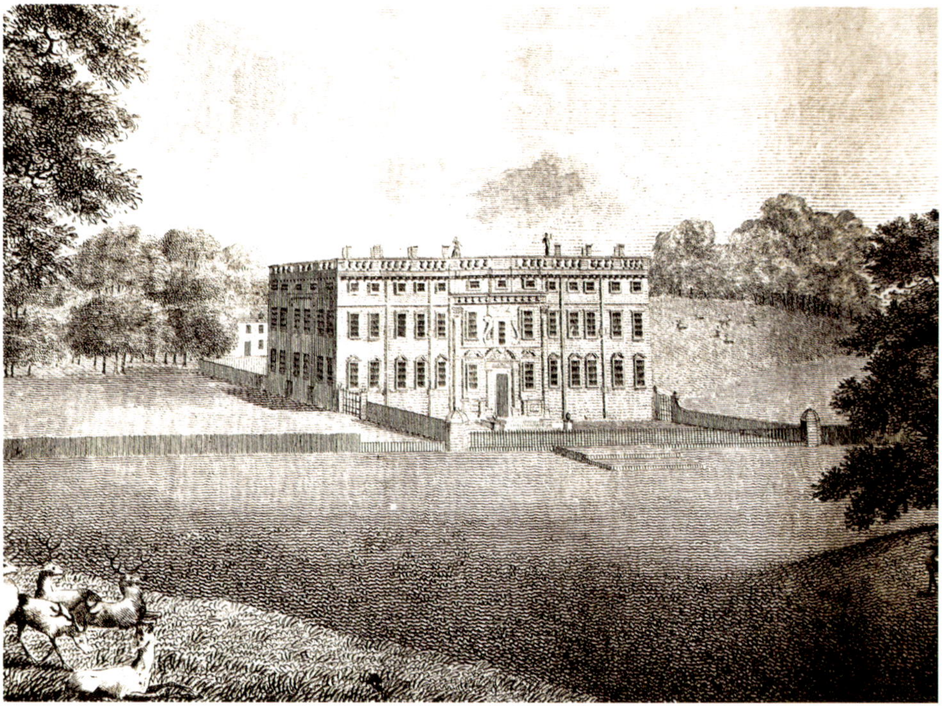

Thoresby, seen from the south-west. From an engraving of 1745. (Private collection)

three-bay attached Corinthian portico, with a flat roof behind a balustraded parapet decorated with statues and set off by a tall lantern flanked by cupolas, probably banqueting houses. The returns were of six paired bays. As built (and completed only in 1687 for the marquess's nephew, the 3rd Lord Kingston), the top storey appears to have been reduced to an attic and the lantern and cupolas elided, attested by an early eighteenth-century vignette, although the possibility is that this is inaccurate and merely records the loss of the then unfashionable roof furnishings. The same year that Evelyn, 2nd Duke of Kingston, was fighting Bonnie Prince Charlie at Culloden, this magnificent pile burned down. It was not replaced until twenty years afterwards.

16. Worksop Manor, 1761

The mid-eighteenth century seems to have been a bad time for major country house fires in Nottinghamshire, as in 1761 another spectacular house burned to the ground: the Earl of Shrewsbury's Worksop Manor. The Talbot family had owned the estate since the fourteenth century, and it was in the previous house, dating from 1530, that Mary, Queen of Scots, was lodged in 1568. In 1585–88 a new prodigy house was built on the same site for George, 6th Earl of Shrewsbury, designed by Robert Smythson. It was tall, one pile deep and wide with varying levels, between three and five storeys, flanked by two-storey almost circular towers on two-storey plinths with projecting bays set in from the angles of two

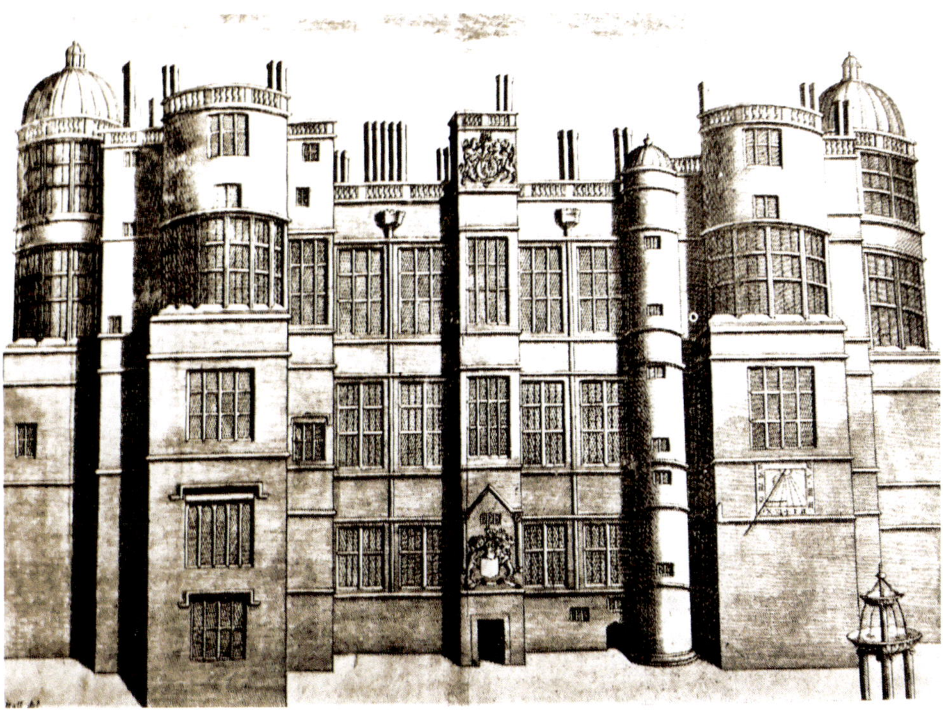

Worksop Manor, seen more or less as it was built, *c.* 1675, from Thoroton. (M. Craven)

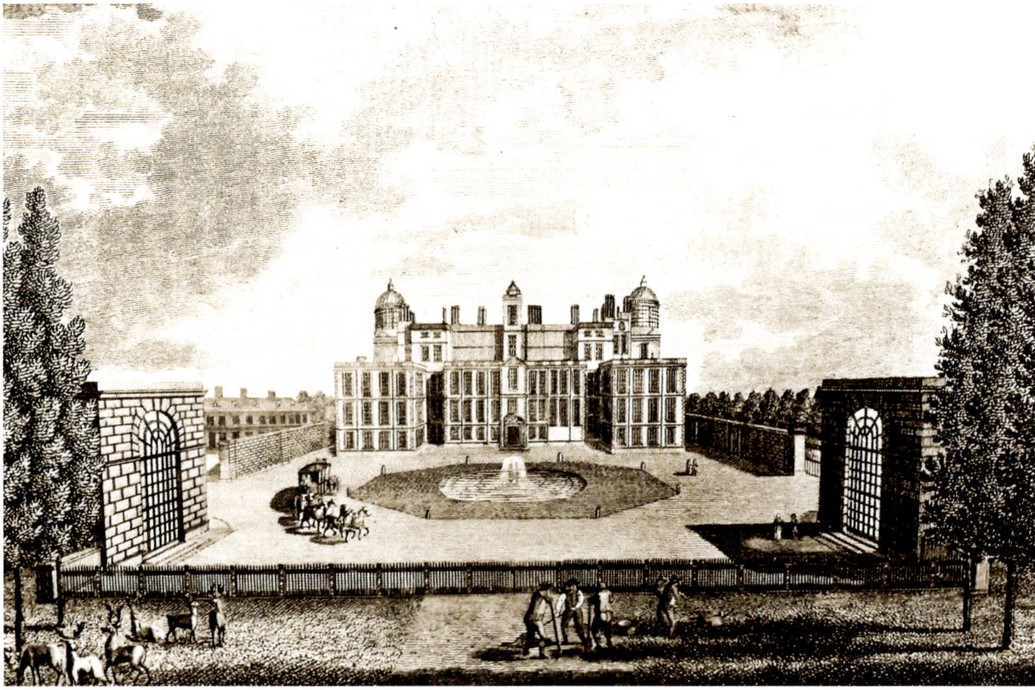

Worksop Manor rebuilt entrance front, from Throsby. (M. Craven)

and three storeys supporting two-storey curved bays, top balustrades and a forest of chimneys on the roof. Like Hardwick (Derbyshire), the long gallery was on the top floor to maximise views. The house passed a generation later to the Duke of Norfolk, whose descendants retained both house and estate until 1840. In 1701, this colossal house was almost doubled in size by the 8th Duke, with the addition of two three-storey, four-bay projecting wings at each angle; the central nine bays were moved forward; and the four towers largely made rectangular, only those at each end retaining one storey of circularity, loosing much of its architectural subtlety. The two stages are well illustrated in Thoroton's history (1677 after Wenceslaus Hollar) and Throsby's revision of it (1797 as it was immediately pre-fire). In 1761, a room was left open to air, but a spark began a fire which was not noticed for two days, after which, having been fanned by a brisk wind, the house was totally destroyed to the value of £100,000 (equivalent to £10.25 million today).

17. Brunsell Hall, Car Colston (II), 1769

Wiltshire-born Revd Prebendary Samuel Brunsell DD (1619–88), uncle by marriage of Sir Christopher Wren, purchased a modest estate here from the Thorotons in 1660 and an adjoining parcel from the recusant Richard Kirke. On the latter, in 1660, he built an H-plan brick mansion of two storeys under a hipped and sprocketed roof. This, and the living of Bingham, was inherited

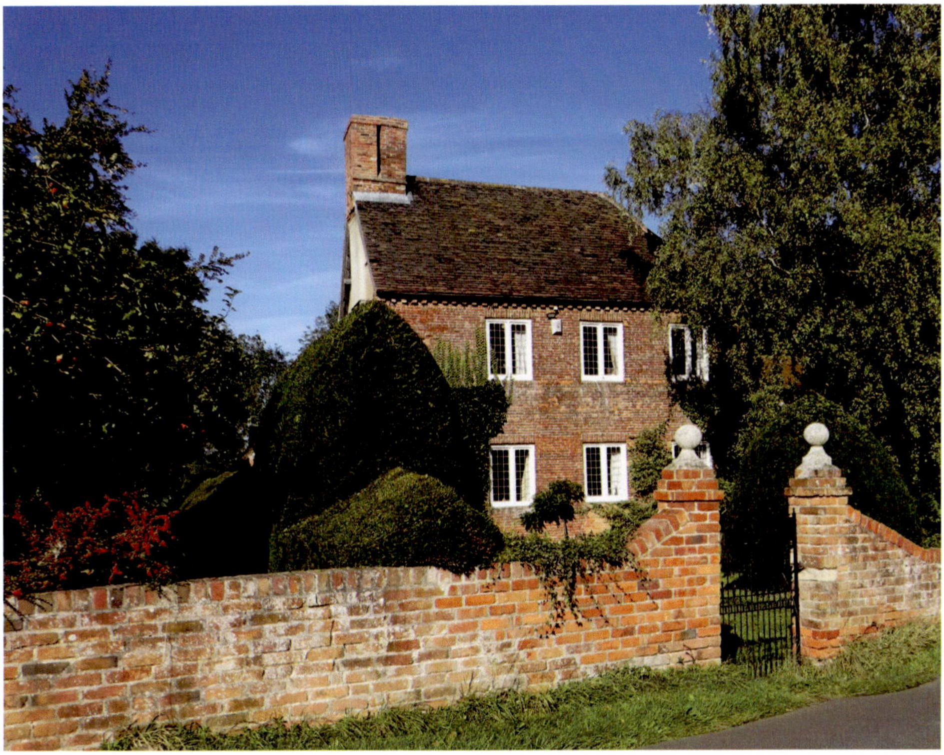

Brunsell Hall, the surviving portion, seen from the lane, October 2023. (M. Craven)

by his son, Henry. Amusingly, an article on the Transactions of the Thoroton Society informs us that Dr Brunsell, then rector of Screveton, was the last man to formally (and successfully) 'lay' a ghost. The property and estate passed early in the next century to the Blaggs, who in 1769 reduced the house by more than two-thirds but retained the land and thenceforth lived elsewhere. The remaining L-plan fragment thereupon was adapted as farm cottages, but has since become a single house again, giving few clues to its grander origins, although inside there remains much fine wainscotting. The boundary wall and entrance had been rebuilt since the bucolic 1905 photograph which appeared in the Transactions of the Thoroton Society and the setting has become somewhat more bosky.

18. Haughton (SAM), 1770

The site of yet another great Nottinghamshire lost house is today occupied by a farmhouse, while nearby stands a notable duck decoy (the oldest in England) and the ruins of what had once been the domestic chapel of the great house at Haughton, dedicated to St James. The house, built by the Holles family within a moated site, once stood in a park (created in 1509) of 900 acres. Held at Domesday by Roger de Poitou, the estate had passed by the fourteenth century to the de Longvilliers, from whom it came to the Maulovels of Rampton and thence to the Stanhopes (see Rampton, p. 17). They sold it in 1537 to Sir William Holles, Lord Mayor of London in 1539. He rebuilt the Stanhopes' house in 1545 (dated on the fabric), much expanded by his convivial younger son, William, whose grandson was created Earl of Clare (Suffolk). He had a scheme to replace the house drawn up by John Smythson, but which was seemingly never built. Thanks to the 2nd Earl marrying the heiress of the Cavendish Duke of Newcastle, his younger son (also married to a Cavendish) was created Duke of Newcastle (on Tyne) but died in 1711. The estate passed to his nephew, Thomas Pelham, who was made Earl of Clare and Duke of Newcastle, but he also died without issue. The estate then passed to his nephew by marriage, Henry Clinton, Earl of Lincoln, who was created Duke of Newcastle (under Lyme). The Holles's house, as depicted by Kip and Knyff's *Britannia Illustrata* in 1707, was irregular, built

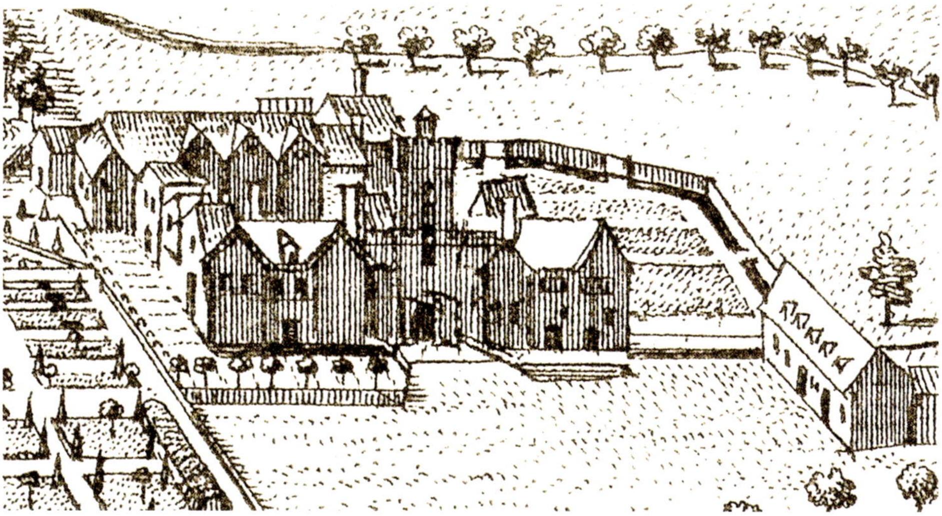

Haughton, as drawn by Leonard Knyff, from *Britannia Illustrata*, 1709. (M. Craven)

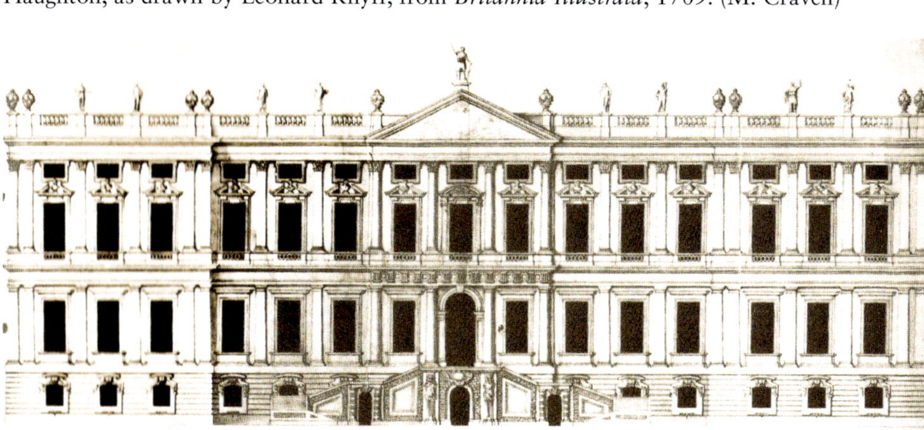

Haughton, the intended new house main front, from *Vitruvius Britannicus*. (Late Edward Saunders)

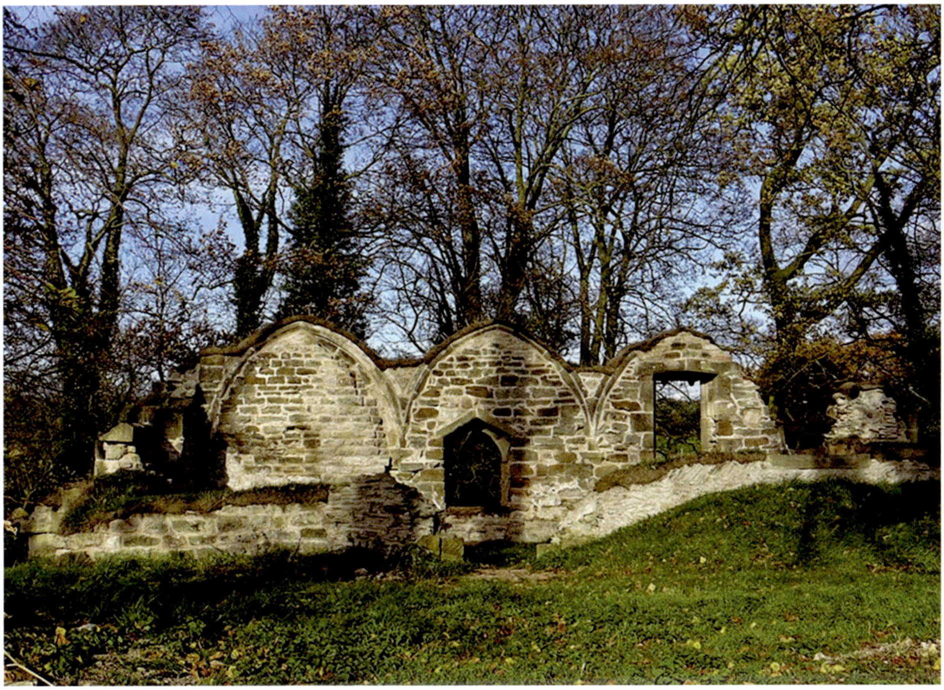

Haughton, surviving fabric of the domestic chapel, 2018. (N. Theasby, Creative Commons)

around a substantial courtyard with a towered gatehouse and surrounded by various gabled ranges seemingly of various dates. The earl had been in two minds whether to build a new house here or at Welbeck, and in 1703 William Talman (again) draw up a scheme for a fifteen-bay pedimented three-storey palace that would have made Chatsworth seem restrained. In the end, it was built at neither place, but his successors opted for living at Welbeck over Haughton and, from 1770, when the family finally moved to newly completed Clumber, the old house was abandoned and largely demolished, Throsby reporting that the remains were in 'total decay' by 1797. (Note that the engraving published in Philip Jones's book (2006) as Haughton is in fact of the ruined house of the dukes of Beford at Houghton Conquest, Bedfordshire.)

19. East Leake Manor, 1785

There were once three manorial estates at East Leake, of which the principal one (close to the church) was held by the Shirleys. Today it is largely overlain by the Old Hall Farm complex. Joyce's manor was originally where the buildings of the former Brookside Farm now stand, but the name was transferred by John Bley to his grand new house on Main Street – years later this became a shop and post office, which only closed in 2003 – and Cosby's manor, latterly a farmhouse demolished in 1963 when Salisbury Avenue was built, and which stood approximately where a block of flats was built in 2006. The foremost family in the early days and throughout the Middle Ages were the Leekes or Leakes (descendants of an eleventh-century Norse settler). They occupied what later became (by inheritance, along with Staunton Harold, Leicestershire) the property of the Shirley family of Derbyshire. By this time there appears to have been a moated manor house, probably of fourteenth-century date. In 1700, Robert Shirley, 1st Earl Ferrers, sold the manorial estate to Sir Thomas Parkyns of Bunny, 2nd Bt (the 'Wrestling baronet'), who demolished the old mansion and proceeded in 1704 to erect a brick and stone house within the moat to his own eccentric design, locally called 'the glass house', being generously, if eccentrically, lit. On the façade was inscribed: 'Hasce Ædis Excogitabuit Delinearuit et Operariis non modo Quotidie Interfuit Verum Etiam praefuit quasi archetectus Thomas Parkyns 2dus Gentis suae Baronettas. AD. 1704' (Thomas Parkyns, 2nd Bt of his family, contrived and drew this house and not only was daily present with the workmen, but also superintended as architect. AD 1704). However, the house found little use by the family and was probably never fitted out, lying empty until in 1785 Sir Thomas's son, the 3rd Bt, demolished it, selling the materials for local reuse.

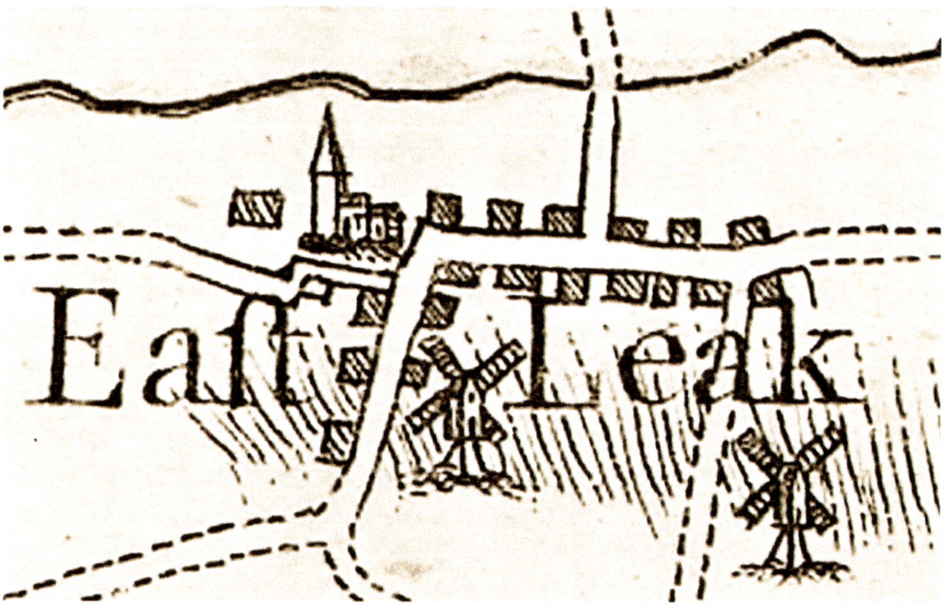

East Leake. The house is represented by the rectangle to the left of the church spire. (Private collection)

20. Headon Hall, 1796

Headon Hall (located south-east of Retford), was an early sixteenth-century house of the Wasteney family, set in a contemporary park. The Tudor house had been rebuilt by Sir Hardolph Wasteneys, 4th Bt and MP, in 1710, who also laid out the park with a number of impressive avenues. On his death without male issue in 1742, the house became largely redundant, his niece and heiress having married into the Suttons of Averham, and was eventually pulled down in 1796. The parkland survives to some extent, including a single surviving avenue, the remnants of the sixteenth-century park pale, some eighteenth-century planting and associated buildings.

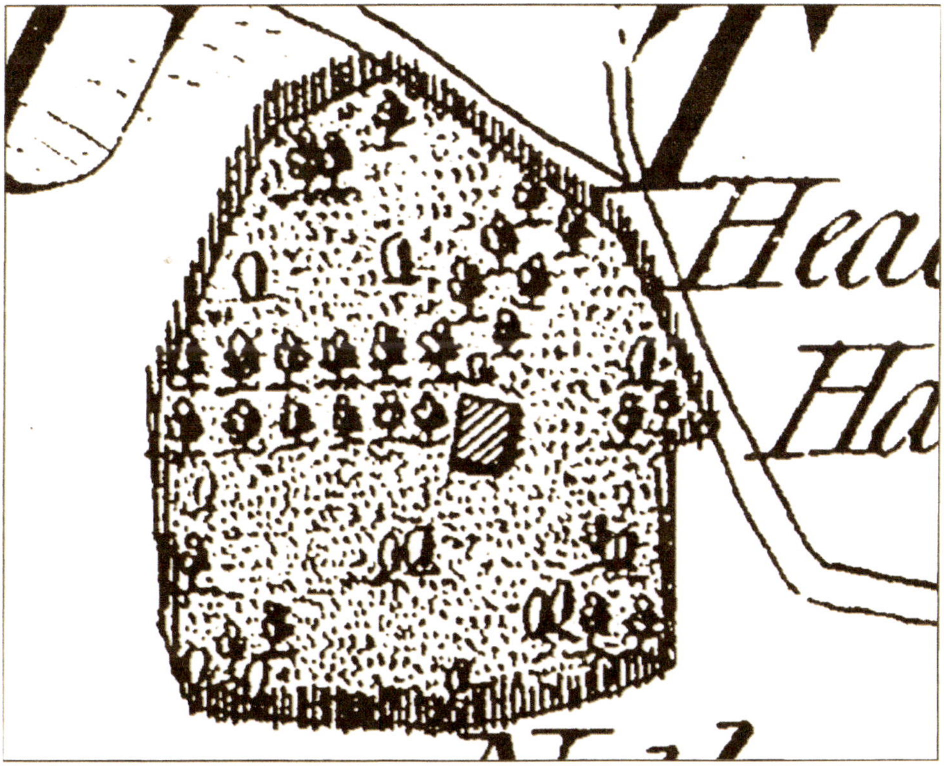

Headon Hall. The site and setting is from Chapman's map of 1774. (Private collection)

Section Three

Losses 1800–99

21. Scofton Hall, 1800

The Jessop family of Broom Hall, near Sheffield, acquired the estate at Scofton towards the close of the sixteenth century, along with a late fourteenth-century house. In the following century the estate passed to the Banks family via an heiress, Joseph Banks MP being listed as in residence there in 1702 – he was probably the man who had built the house a few years before. It was sold in 1727 to General Richard Sutton of Kelham, who built a relatively modest new house there. It was of five bays, two storeys with attic dormers in a sprocketed roof. Robert Sutton of Scofton (1699–1776) is said to have made improvements while his grandson, R. W. E. Sutton sold it in 1796 to Francis Foljambe of Osberton. He had no use for the house itself and demolished it in 1800 and amalgamated the pleasure grounds, with those adjacent belonging to Osberton Hall, thus explaining the reason for his purchase. The notably extensive mid-eighteenth-century kitchen garden walls survive. In 1830–33 his grandson built the present church of St John the Evangelist across the lake from Osberton Hall, on the site of the former house.

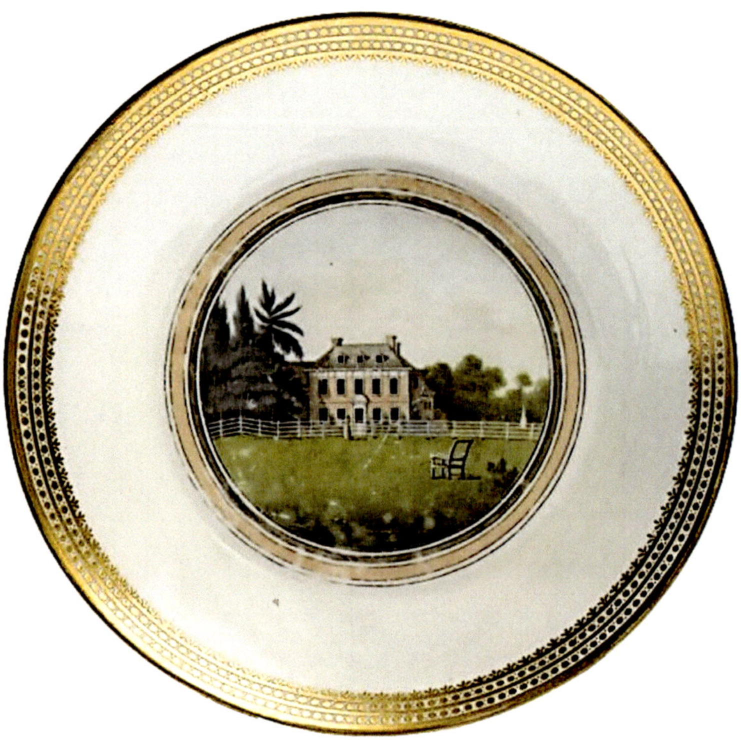

Scofton Hall as built, shown painted on a Pinxton plate. (Mellors & Kirk)

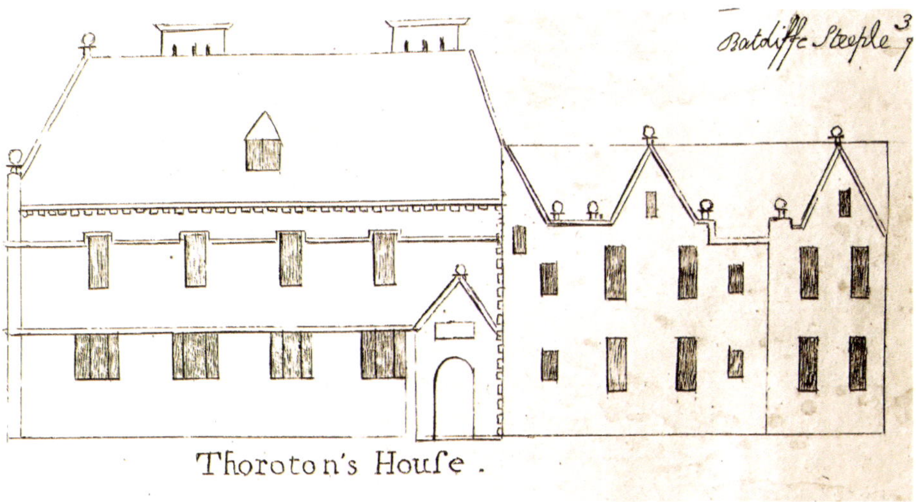

Car Colston, Thoroton's House (left), incorporating Toke Place (right), *c.* 1675, from Throsby. (M. Craven)

22. Car Colston Old Hall, 1812

The old hall at Car Colston was originally two houses: Moryn Hall, inherited by the Thorotons from the Moryns *c.* 1380 and Toke Hall, built by Colonel Hacker in around 1640. While the latter had a three-gabled façade of eight bays, ball finials and matching returns, no hint of the appearance of the Thoron's house as survived. However, Robert Thoroton, the father of the county's historian, acquired both and, while keeping much of Toke Hall, replaced his own house with a large extension to Toke Hall to form the Old Hall. This consisted of a two-storey four-bay façade under a high hipped roof with a single attic dormer, with string courses above the three-light mullioned windows on the ground floor and the single casements on the first. There was a timber modillion cornice and quadruple chimney stacks. A gabled porch acted as the main entry where the two buildings joined. The upper storey windows and most of those on the early seventeenth-century part were later replaced by sashes, with the string course cranked up over them. The posterity of Dr Thoroton's grandson, Philip Sherard, died out and the estate came to the More-Molyneux family of Loseley, Surrey. The house was derelict when John Throsby drew it, and was demolished in 1812 and replaced by a bland three bay two-and-a-half-storey stuccoed Regency farmhouse incorporating some fragments of its predecessor.

23. Kirketon Hall, Screveton, 1824

Richard Whalley MP (d. 1583) lived in the house, which was adjacent to Screveton Church, which his family had inherited from the Kirketons via the Leeks. His descendant, Peniston Whalley, sold it to Thomas Thoroton (son of the historian's brother) in 1685 and he seems to have renamed it Screveton Hall and whose posterity had made considerable alterations by 1793. In 1824 it was purchased by a Thoroton relative, Colonel Thomas Hildyard, who demolished it and donated

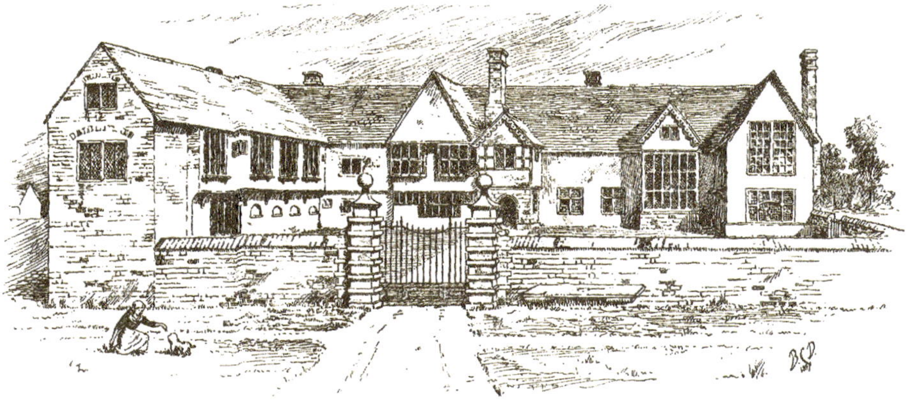

Kirketon Hall entrance front. (Private collection)

the land to the church. There are views of it in three stages of development: the oldest, in the council's collections, showing an irregular centrally recessed old house of much charm. Two further views, published in the Proceedings of the Thoroton Society, show the entrance front rebuilt in late Elizabethan mode with deep mullion and transom windows and an additional rather grand cross-wing. The other shows the same front with the left cross-wing replaced by a four-bay two-storey addition of *c*. 1680/1710, and the right-hand cross-wing rebuilt higher with an attic Diocletian window and enclosed by a plain giant order, presumably effected after around 1760.

24. Owthorpe Hall, 1825

Owthorpe Hall came into the possession of the Hutchinsons by purchase in the sixteenth century. Sir Thomas Hutchinson, who was High Sheriff in 1620, also much expanded the estate, becoming the owner of the entire manor. His successor, the Parliamentary commander Colonel John Hutchinson, occupied his post-Civil War years (prior to his arrest as a signatory of Charles I's death warrant)

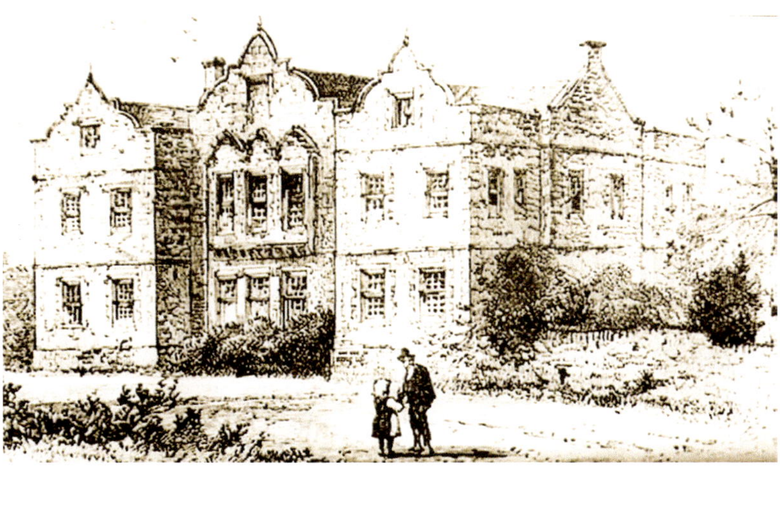

Owthorpe Hall from the south-east. (Private collection)

by building a new house seven bays wide of two storeys with attics and a recessed centre, all embellished by three shaped gables crowning a trio of corbeled out windows. The returns were of six bays and the house was quite substantial. The through hall had a reception room above it and the oak staircase was said to have been impressive. Colonel Hutchinson's widow sold house and estate to his half-brother Charles, whose posterity resided there, replacing the windows with sashes, until it was sold in 1773 to Sir George Bromley, 2nd Bt of East Stoke. He did not need the house, but it was tenanted for some years by his bailiff, under whom it fell into dereliction. In 1825 it was demolished by Sir Robert Bromley, 3rd Bt.

25. Selston (Old) Hall, 1830

An estate at Selston was purchased by Timothy Pusey (1560–1647), formerly the faithful and efficient private secretary of Bess of Hardwick, who, in his old age, supported the king in the Civil War, receiving a posthumous pardon from Parliament. The house, of stone, had a five-bay central section with steep coped gables, of two storeys and attics, flanked by cross-wings in similar style. It had an old-style great hall to the left of the offset entrance, which had a single similar-storey balustraded portico. The fenestration was of mullion and transom cross type, with two-light mullions to the attics. Pusey's daughter and ultimate co-heiress transmitted the estate to William Willoughby of Aston (Oxfordshire) and from his posterity, divided, it came to Lord Melbourne and Lady Dixie by the end of the eighteenth century. The Dixie baronets, who retained much of the estate well into the twentieth century, vacated the house in the early nineteenth century, drastically reduced it and rebuilt a remaining portion as a simple farmhouse, which retained a fine oak staircase. After the Second World War this was

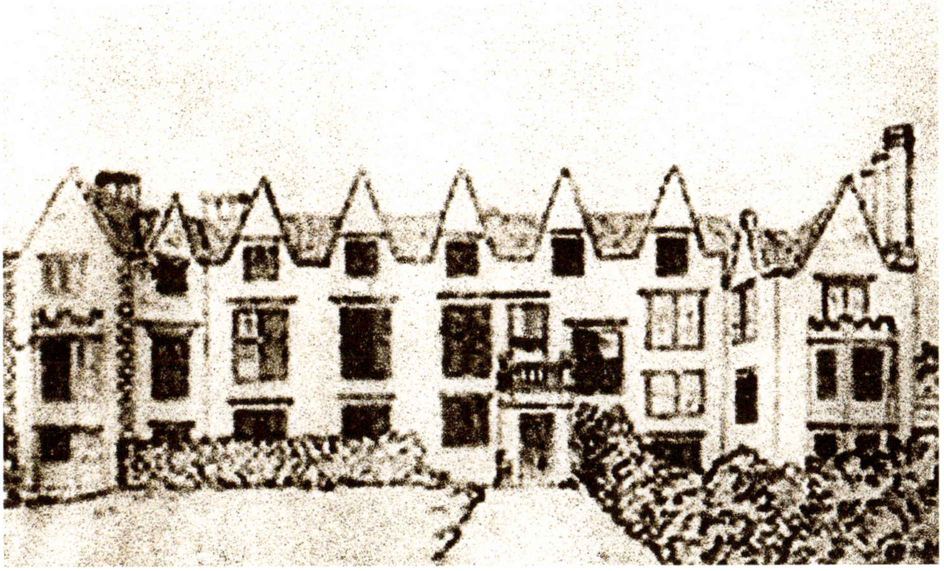

Selston Hall, *c.* 1775. (Private collection)

also allowed to fall into dereliction, being finally cleared in 1976 to be replaced by a new structure entirely which retained the staircase. A pair of rusticated stone gate piers of circular section with ball finials (very John Smythson-like) were noted on-site a century ago, along with some walling, but are not discoverable today.

26. Muskham House, North Muskham, 1840

Banker and prolific amateur architect Joseph Pocklington (1736–1817) became the lessee of a modest prebendal estate at North Muskham in 1775. Having rebuilt one house (see North Muskham Grange, p. 73), he decided in 1793 to build a fresh residence for himself nearby on the water meadows of the Trent which he named Muskham House. Throsby called it 'one of the most spacious and commodious houses possessed by any private gentleman in the county', but in truth it was an awkward exercise in late Palladianism. Of two storeys over a rustic, with a pedimented three-bay centre and single-storey bays at each end, all the fenestration (except in the rustic) was Serlian, a favourite motif of his, being especially prevalent in the three eccentric houses he designed for his Derwentwater estate (snootily deplored by Wordsworth and Coleridge). It was set in a small park and it is where he died in 1817, financially unscathed apparently by the failure of the family bank in Newark in 1809. By 1832 estate was held by the (Webb) Edges of Strelley and the house was unoccupied; consequently, in 1839–40 it was completely demolished, leaving only one of the two lodge cottages still standing at the entrance to the drive from the Great North Road.

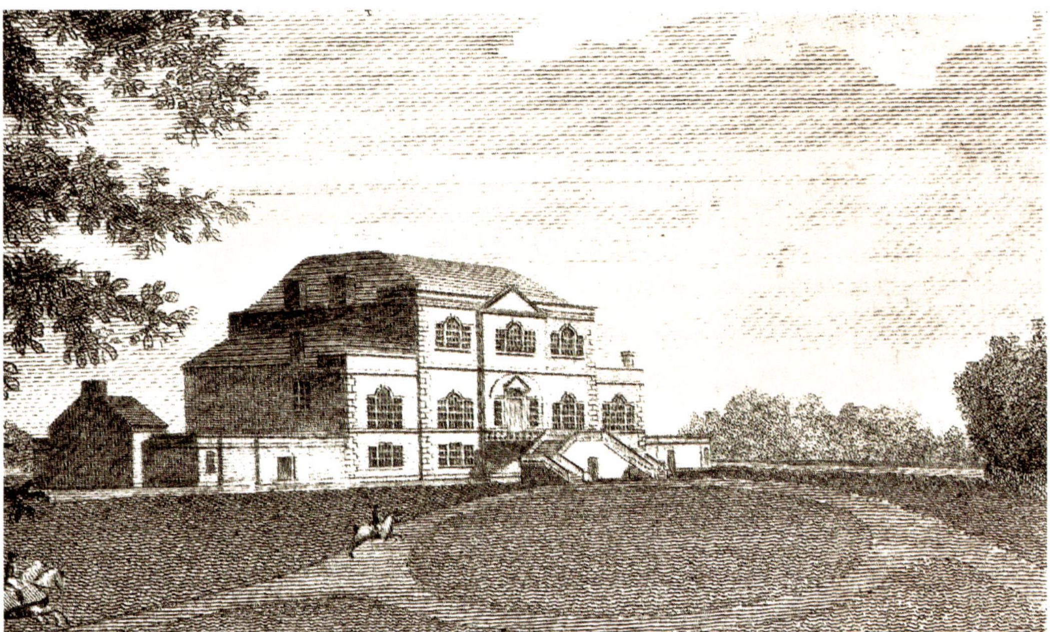

Muskham House, North Muskham, 1793. (M. Craven)

27. Worksop Manor, 1841

Following its total destruction by fire in 1761, the Duke of Norfolk, later that same year, commissioned James Paine to design a replacement for the burnt-out Elizabethan mansion. He planned an approximately square Palladian house with a

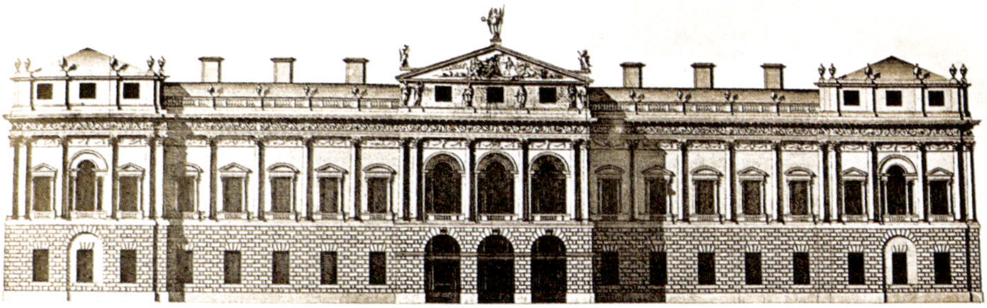

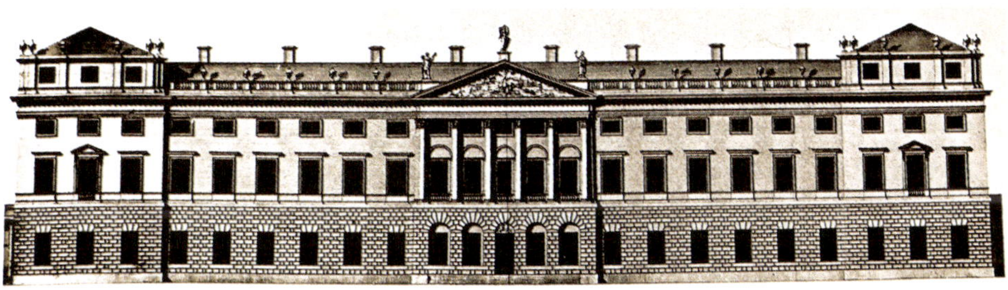

Worksop Manor with Paine's elevations. From the 1767 edition of *Plans, elevations and sections of Noblemen and Gentlemen's Houses*. (M. Craven)

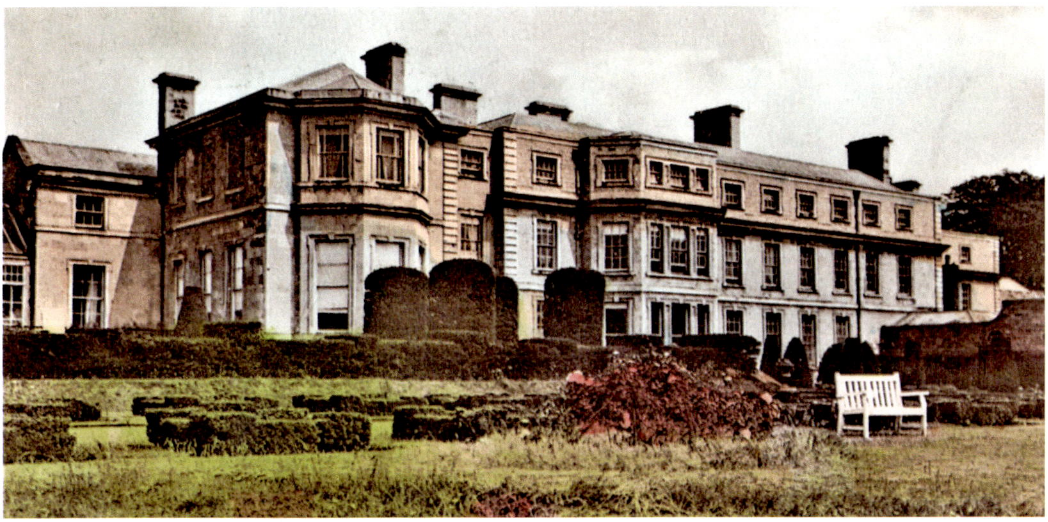

The remaining east range of Worksop Manor. From a colour-printed postcard postmarked 1954. (M. Craven)

vast hall around a central courtyard, which would have been one of the largest houses ever built in England had it been completed. However, only the west wing had been finished when work stopped on the house in 1767 on the death of the duke's only son, but even this was on a palatial scale: twenty-one bays, a *piano nobile* over a rustic with attic storey and further attics in the three bay-end pavilions, all centered on a five-bay pedimented element with arched fenestration to the first floor. On the death of the 9th Duke in 1777, the estate passed to a distant cousin, aged fifty-seven and living in Surrey. Neither he nor his immediate successors lived at Worksop, and it became neglected. The 12th Duke gave it to his son, the Earl of Surrey, in 1815. In 1838, Lord Surrey sold the estate to the Duke of Newcastle of nearby Clumber Park for £375,000. He ruthlessly stripped the house. He demolished the main wing with gunpowder, having sold off the roof lead and some fittings, as he was only interested in adding the land to his own estate. However, the remainder – the unfinished north range, the east stable range and the south family range – were all suffered to remain; indeed, the south range was adapted as reasonably spacious living quarters. In 1890 the 7th Duke sold the house and its 2,000 acres to Nottingham brewer Alderman Sir John Robinson JP (1850–1929), on whose death it was inherited by his great-nephew John Farr, among whose posterity it remains.

28. Kelham Hall, 1857

Kelham was anciently the estate of the Suttons of Averham, who built a seventeenth-century house, home to the diplomat Robert, 2nd Lord Lexinton PC, whose daughter and heiress married 3rd Duke of Rutland in 1717 and who died

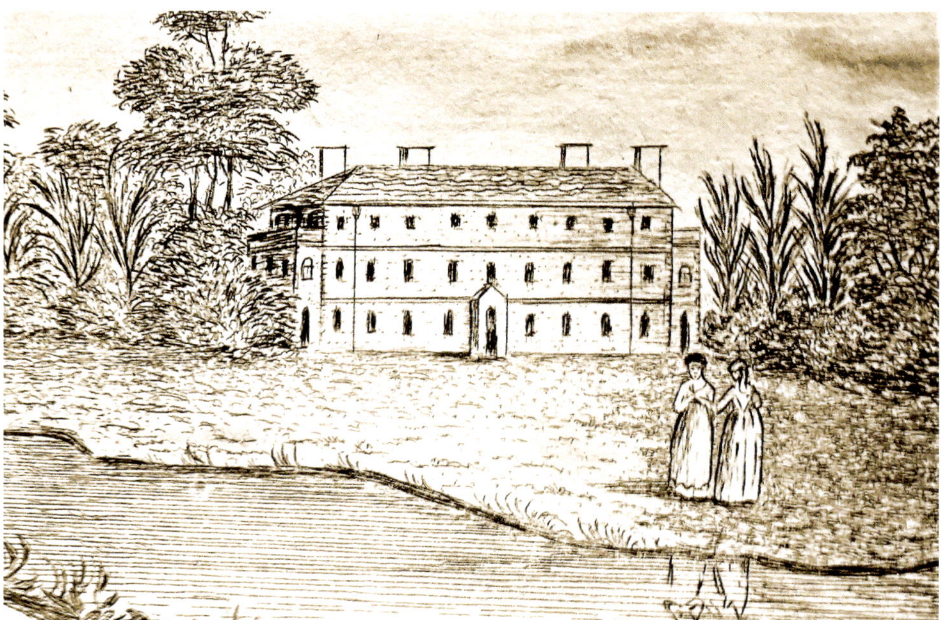

Kelham Hall, from Throsby, 1797. (M. Craven)

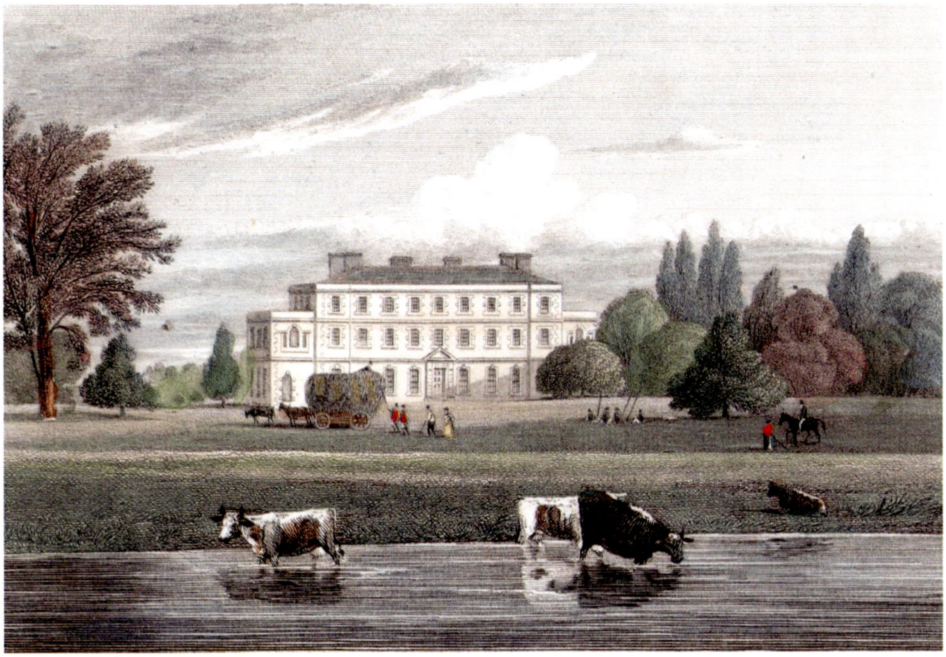

Kelham Hall. From a hand-coloured engraving by J. P. Neal, 1829. (M. Craven)

in 1723. His executors were charged with rebuilding the house for the intended use of the duke's second son, Lord Robert Manners-Sutton, on whom the estate was settled. They were responsible for engaging the young and largely untried London architect John Sanderson (d. 1774), who built a substantial new brick house, which was completed in 1731. The house was four-square and of three storeys under a hipped roof and nine bays wide, the end bays breaking slightly forward. A later two-storey bay was added to the west with superimposed Serlian windows, and the park was extensively landscaped. In 1843 John Henry Manners-Sutton (1822–98) commissioned Anthony Salvin to add a Jacobethan service wing, a Restoration-style balustraded roof walk and he re-faced the main front in ashlar. Fifteen years later, towards the end of some less substantial modifications overseen by Sir Gilbert Scott, a contractor's spark set the house on fire and it was totally destroyed, leaving Sir Gilbert a free hand to start again to build the present, vividly Gothic (but never really completed) house, which was sold by the family with the remains of the estate in 1973.

29. Thoresby, 1868

Following the destruction by fire of his house in 1746 (see p. 20), Evelyn Pierrepont, 2nd Duke of Kingston KG, seems not to have been inclined to replace his house. Yet at the age of fifty-six, he plucked up courage, marshalled his resources and began again. He commissioned John Carr of York in 1767 to design him a conventionally Palladian house of two storeys over a rustic, the main front seven bays wide, articulated by a three-bay pediment decorated with urns

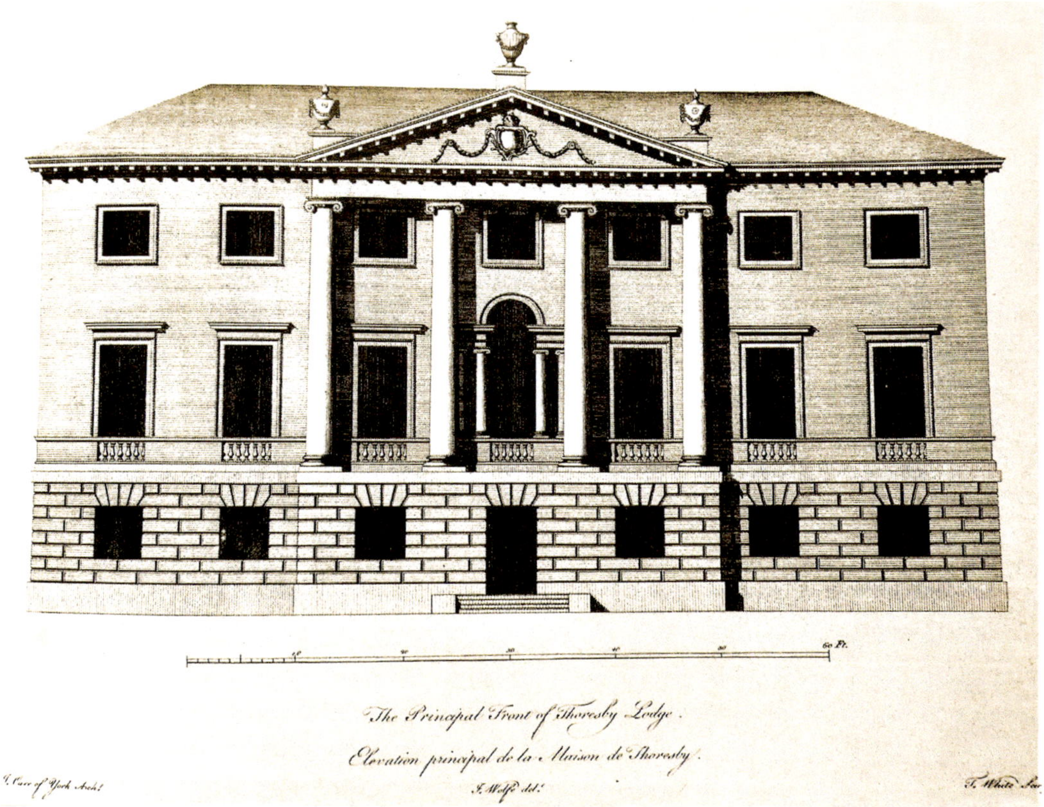

Thoresby II's elevation by J. Wolfe. From *Vitruvius Britannicus*. (Late Edward Saunders)

supported by a tetrastyle Ionic attached order centered by a Serian window on the *piano nobile*. It was all under a hipped roof, and the pediment had neo-classical swags in the tympanum and urns above. The garden front had a full-height, canted bay and the six bay returns were perfectly austere. There were stables to the west forming a courtyard. It was completed 1771, so the duke had but eighteen months to enjoy it prior to his death in 1773. On the death of the duchess in 1788 the estate devolved upon her nephew, Charles Medows (later Pierrepont), later 1st Earl Manvers. Sydney, 3rd Earl Manvers, decided Carr's house too modest for him, and he commissioned Anthony Salvin to build the present house on a fresh site, and in 1868 it was unceremoniously demolished.

30. Skegby Manor (II and SAM), *c.* 1875

The remains of the ancient manor house of Skegby are situated on private land (but visible from Mansfield Road) east of the hall, opposite the end of Buttery Lane. The first house was built by Godfrey Spigurnel (sergeant to King John) allegedly in 1207 (and extended almost a century later), being one of only two Norman manor houses surviving in Nottinghamshire (the other is Wansley, see p. 68), although both are in ruins, making them most emphatically lost houses. Godfrey Spigurnel's family remained owners of the manor until 1334 when Elizabeth Spigurnel sold it to Richard Pensax. The manor, much rebuilt and extended in vernacular style, later passed to the Lindleys in 1450 and their posterity remained the owners into the early nineteenth century. Their descendant John Dodsley was the owner at this time, and they remained the proprietors until the 1930s. The house itself slowly became disused as a result of the building of Skegby Hall in the eighteenth century a little further along the road (now flats), although it was still roofed in 1867 when subject of an extant painting. The site was excavated and the ruins consolidated in 1983.

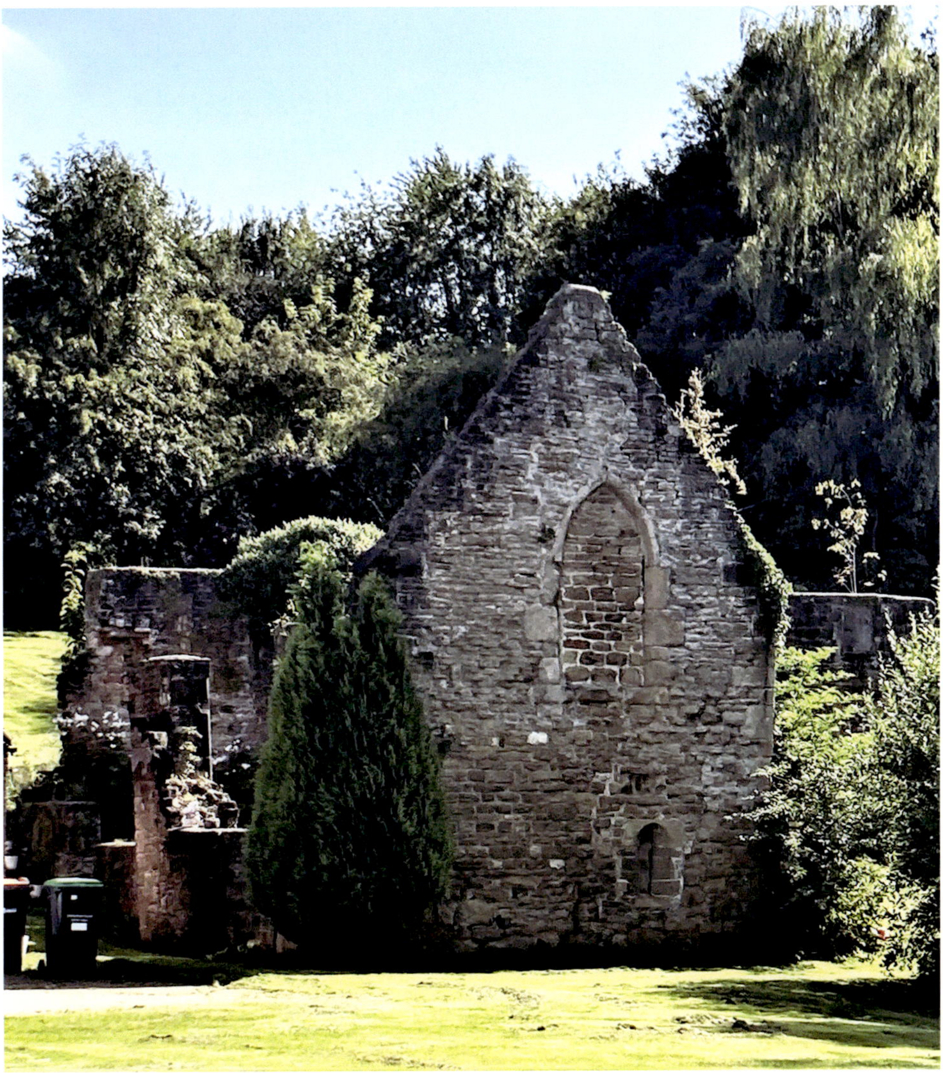

The remains of Skegby Manor House, from the road, September 2023. (M. Craven)

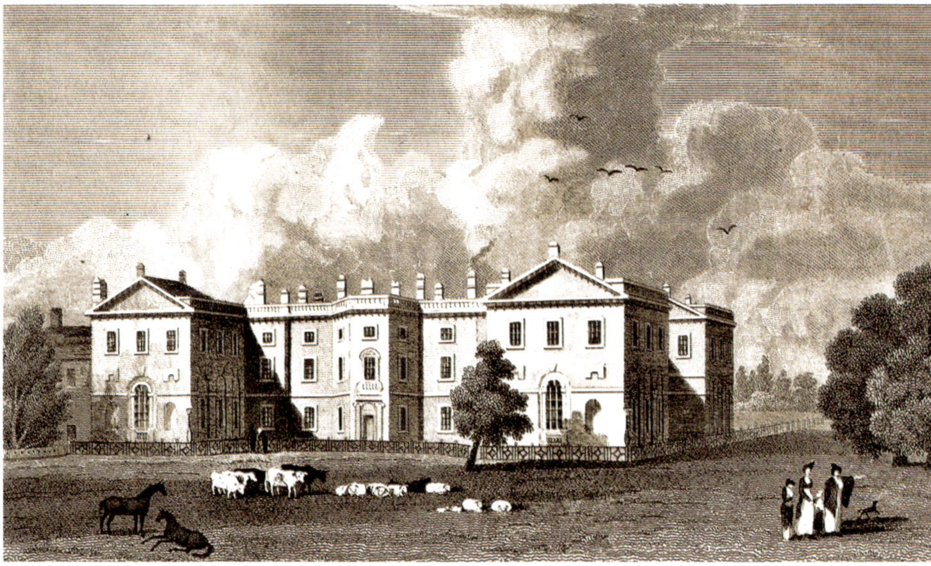

Clumber, Stephen Wright's south front as built. The garden is fenced rather than protected by a haha, as was more usual at the time. Engraving by J. P. Neale, 1808. (M. Craven)

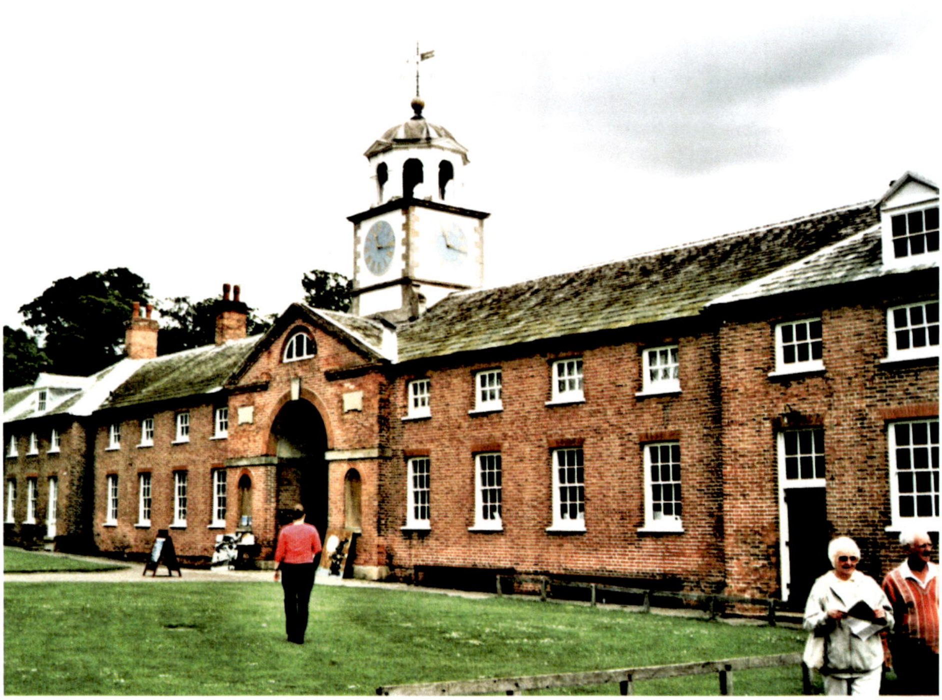

West front of Clumber's stable block, photographed in 1986. The turret clock and sundial are by John Whitehurst FRS, whom the client, the Duke of Newcastle, made a stamper of the money weights at the Royal Mint. (M. Craven)

31. Clumber Park, 1879

This part of Sherwood Forest was in the hands of Newstead Priory until 1568, when it was granted to the Taverners and from them passed to the Holles family of Haughton. By 1707, John Holles, Earl of Clare and Duke of Newcastle, had built a hunting lodge on the site of the later house and had enclosed over 3,000 acres of parkland. His successor but one, also Duke of Newcastle (of the 3rd creation), inherited in 1768 and commissioned Palladian architect Stephen Wright (a pupil of William Kent) to build a very fine classical house. The park was transformed (with only a brief consultation from Lancelot Brown) by the addition of planned landscape and a fine lake, conceivably by William Emes, whose friend John Whitehurst FRS of Derby installed flushing lavatories, back boiler-heated running water, clocks and a sundial. Park buildings (notably the bridge) by Wright and John Simpson survive. The house had a chequered career. Benjamin Dean Wyatt made alterations in 1814, and Sir Robert Smirke in 1829, including the duke's library and (almost) detached study, which latter survives as the café. Then, on 26 March 1879, disaster struck: the house was gutted by a serious fire and required a rebuild that virtually amounted to a new house.

32. Sneinton Manor, 1894

Sneinton Manor House was long a subsidiary seat of the earls and dukes of Kingston and later of the earls Manvers, the Pierreponts having acquired the estate from the de Tibetots in the fourteenth century. The stone house dated from the mid-seventeenth century, being of two piles, of two storeys and attics, with coped gables. There was a substantial cross-wing at the east end, and the fenestration was of mullion and transom cross type separated by sting courses. The two-light

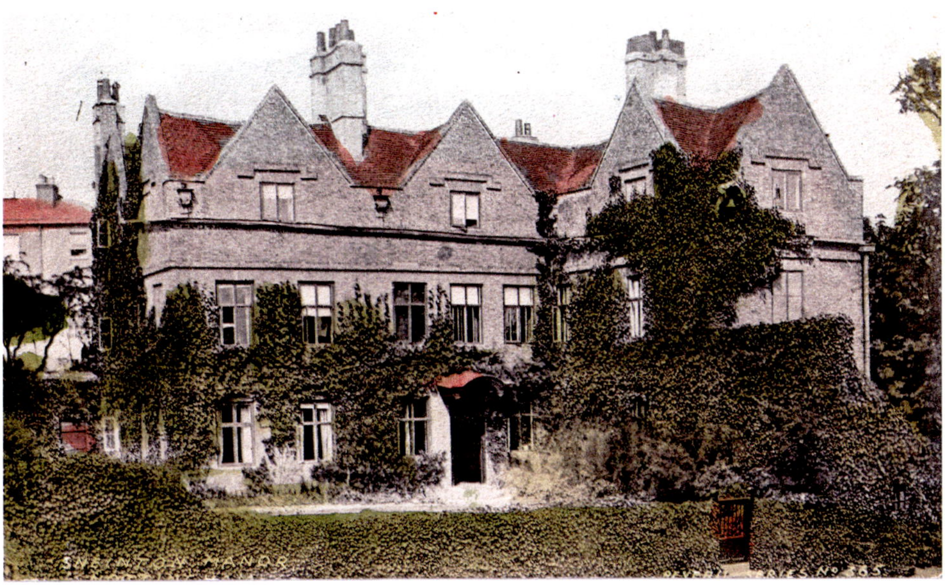

Sneinton Manor, from a chromolithographic postcard of 1906. (James Darwin)

mullioned attic windows in the gables were ensigned by cranked hood moulds, but the façade was later marred by injudicious positioning of rainwater goods. In the 1760s Samuel Morley, a yeoman farmer, was cultivating land around the manor house while at the same time becoming interested in the growing trade of hosiery manufacture. His son John was born at the manor in 1768, followed seven years later by his brother Richard. Samuel Morley died in 1776, but his sons abandoned the land (though retained the house) in favour of hosiery and made a substantial fortune. Arthur, the last of the Morleys, died in 1860, being succeeded as tenant by Colonel James Davidson, who died in 1878 and whose widow left in 1888. Finding further tenants for a house in slow decay was too much of a challenge and it was demolished in spring 1894, followed by a sale of materials.

33. Bilby Hall, *c.* 1890

In 1801, when Francis Foljambe of Osberton MP purchased the house and estate at Bilby from Morgan Vane, a grandson of 2nd Lord Barnard, the house appeared fairly substantial with a two-storey Georgianised hall range with, to the left, a tall cross-wing embellished by a two-storey canted bay with superimposed Serlianas and a pair of lower gable ends (representing another cross range) to the right, both with substantial stacks rising from their apices – apparently the rebuilding of a Tudor house built by the Levinzes. Vane had enclosed 260 acres of woodland to make a park preserving the best oaks some five years before. A lake was created from the nearby Leen, south-west of the house, overlooked by a Doric temple. His alterations at Osberton complete, Foljambe moved out to be replaced by his daughter-in-law and grandson, George, who lived there until he in turn succeeded to Osberton. After standing untenanted, demolition followed sometime after his death in 1869. The service wing was converted into hunt kennels and stable block became estate cottages.

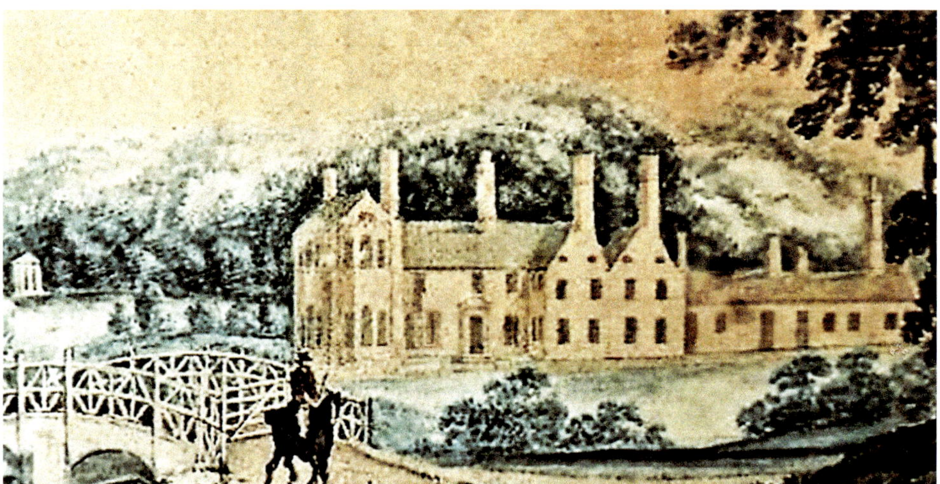

Engraved and hand-coloured view of Bilby Hall, 1798. (Private collection)

Section Four

Losses 1900–45

34. Gilcroft House, Mansfield, 1903

This interesting house appears to have started out as a stone two-storey six-bay-wide William and Mary (or slightly earlier) town villa, with quoins and a two-bay steep central pediment – typical of its era, but the latter feature was unusual in sporting a central square light instead of an armorial or a cartouche – all of *c.* 1689. It is by no means clear for whom it was built, but the suspicion is that it was the home of Robert Brunts, after whom the lane in which the house stood (alas, since cleared away for an avoiding road) was presumably named. He was the son of the 'Mr Robert Brunts' (occasionally Brants or Brunt) who told the heralds in the 1662 *Visitation of Nottinghamshire* that his house had been 'plundered in the wars' during which his proofs of arms were lost. His son Samuel died in 1709, leaving a charity. By around 1780 (leaving a large lacuna in our knowledge of the building) the house was home to William Brodhurst, maltster, who appears to have enlarged it by adding a three-bay wing to the south-east angle, a canted bay to the principal façade and a further extension to the west to the street. On his death in 1846, the son sold to Captain James Salmond JP, but from 1853 it was the property of William Midworth, iron-founder, who died unmarried in 1866.

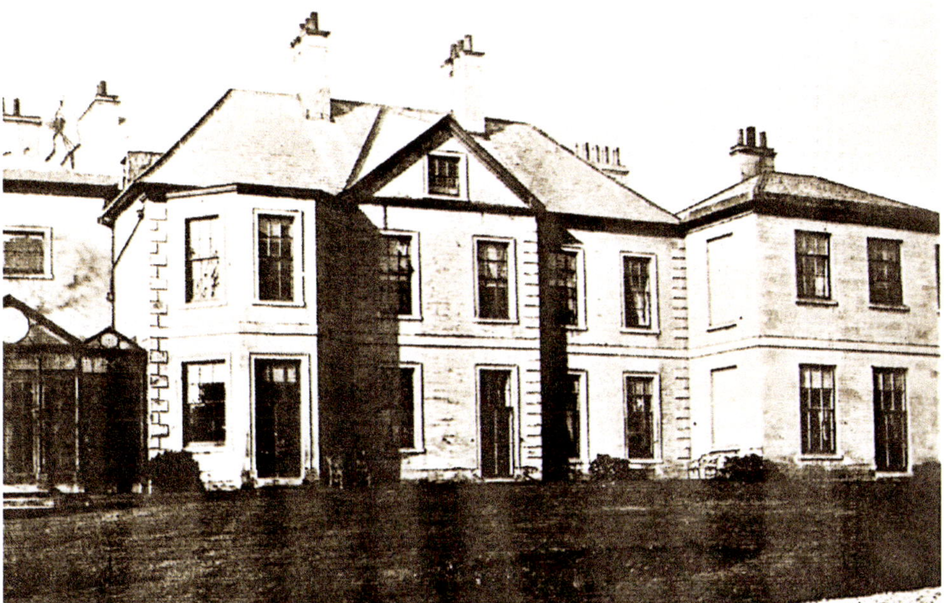

Garden front of Gilcroft House, Mansfield, shortly before demolition. (Our Mansfield)

His sisters lived there until 1884 when they left and let to Addison Titley, a local brewer, there until 1902. The Midworth executors sold the property in 1903 to James Henry Blake, a local ironmonger, who soon afterwards demolished the house and redeveloped part of the site.

35. Chauntry House, Appleton Gate, Newark, 1919

Newark's Chauntry was originally a residence for the priests of one of the chantries of the town's nearby parish church. Post-Reformation it came into the hands of the Leakes of Sutton Scarsdale (Derbyshire) but, like Ashbourne Mansion, it was essentially a country house with park and estate despite its urban setting. In 1681 Robert, 3rd Earl of Scarsdale sold the site and the remaining estate to Samuel Foster, allegedly a 'friend and intimate' of Sir John Vanburgh, although his name seems absent from Sir John's biographies. In Queen Anne's reign he built a new house in 'a sort of Palladian style suggested by Sir John', as one account has it. It had an enriched seven-bay, two-storey façade, in no way Palladian, and far too fussy to justify any attribution to Vanburgh, especially as it included Gibbs surrounds to the fenestration (combined with odd baroque carved lintels), a conceit never employed by him. The Doric portico would appear to have been a Regency-period addition. Foster's heirs sold in 1783 to Joseph Sikes, formerly of St Helen's, Derby, but married to Jane Heron, daughter of a Newark grandee. Sikes employed William Lindley of Doncaster to create neo-classical interiors and his posterity were there until the 1870s when it was occupied successively by a brewer and a maltster, before being purchased in 1919 by the widowed developer Emily Blagg, who peremptorily demolished it to make way for a cinema. A pretty Gothic lodge to the park survived nearby until 1936.

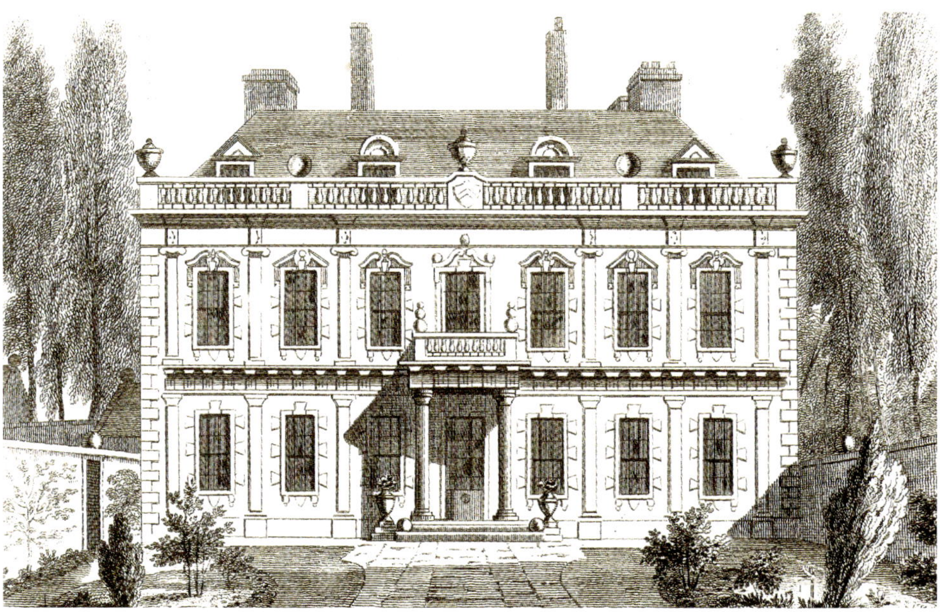

Chauntry House, Newark. (Georgian Group)

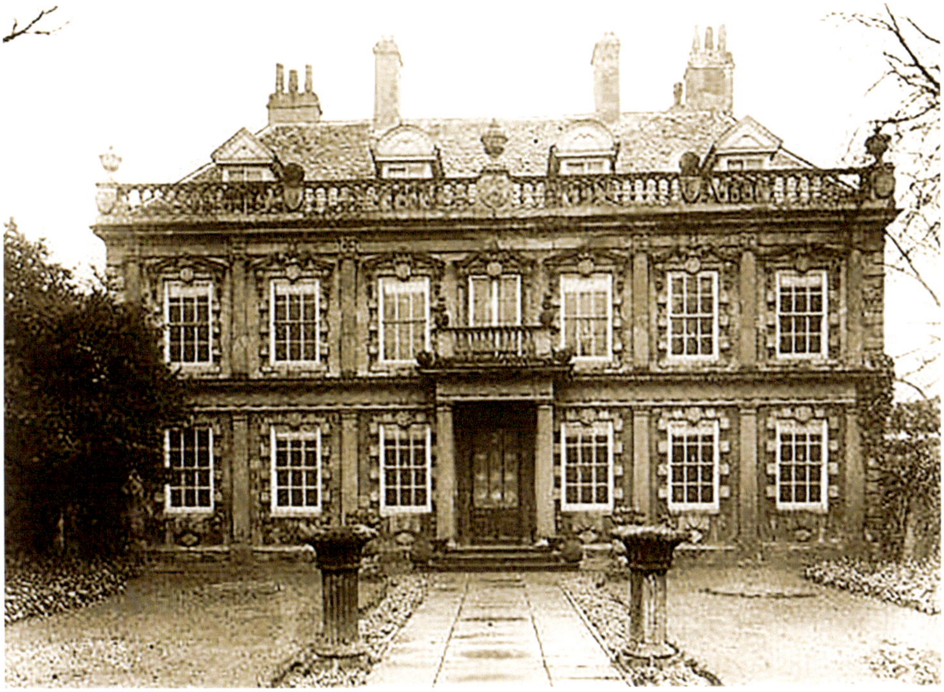

Chauntry House, Newark, *c.* 1900. (Private collection)

36. Sutton Manor, Sutton-in-Ashfield, 1928

The Sutton family held the manorial estate, originally from the king, and Gerard de Sutton later gave the church there to Thurgarton Priory. The estate itself later passed to the FitzRandolphs of Cotes Park, Derbyshire, who are believed to have built a house here in the very early Tudor period. The irregular gables and massive stone attached chimney breasts were typical of the period, and the ashlar walls were penetrated by two-light mullioned windows, but the street front to what later became Devonshire Square had three-light mullions under a pitched roof. The only distinguishing feature inside was apparently the large old-fashioned hearth under a massive stone bressumer, which was made big enough for smoking bacon and allowing room for the ingle-nooks. This particular chimney, however, was pulled down aroundr 1881. The next residents were the Langfords, who succeeded to it by marriage. They appear to have been a cadet branch of the Longfords (*sic*) of Longford, Derbyshire, and who were in residence there until the early eighteenth century and who are thought to have rebuilt the house in the mid-seventeenth century. It seems that they were succeeded by the Brandreths, while in 1838 it was occupied by Mr Beecroft, a farmer, followed before 1873 by Revd and Hon. John Marsham (1842–1926), a younger son of the 3rd Earl of Romney, then rector of Barton Segrave, Northamptonshire. By 1907 the house was occupied by Mr Bishop, Borough Surveyor, but in 1910 town improvements (doubtless promoted by Mr Bishop) necessitated its partial demolition, although according to George Bonser it was not until 1928 that it was cleared away completely.

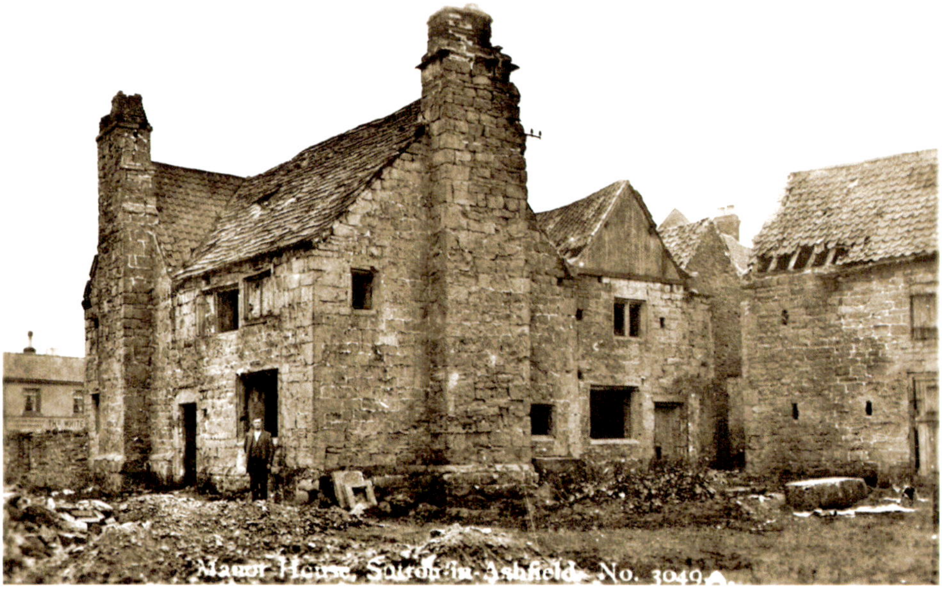

Sutton Manor, Sutton-in-Ashfield. Shown on a postcard under (partial) demolition in 1910. (M. Craven)

37. Chilwell Hall, 1933

Chilwell Hall was a substantial but lowish two-storey stone house built in 1803 and incorporating portions of its predecessor (dated on the fabric 1652). Although largely lacking in ornament, it was adorned with profuse crenellations, presumably the work of a local architect like William Stretton of Nottingham. The entrance was through a later tall lancet arch penetrating a single-storey range linking the projecting end bays of the main façade. The estate came to Sir Peter Martell from the de Chilwells, and from him via Sir William Babington, Chief Justice of the Common Pleas in 1423, to Sir Robert Sheffield. From a drawing in the Smythson collection at the RIBA we learn that Smythson drew an extant plan for a new house *c.* 1585–92 for Edmund, 3rd Lord Sheffield (later 1st Earl of Mulgrave), but it is unclear whether it was built. If it was, 1652 must mark alterations carried out by Thomas Charlton, whose father Nicholas had acquired the estate between 1631 and 1650. The family remained there until Geoffrey Charlton left in 1932, when, there being no takers at the subsequent sale, the estate was broken up and the house demolished in 1933 to make way for housing.

38. Nuthall Temple, 1929

Nuthall was sold to James Ayscough at the beginning of the seventeenth century and from him descended to John Digby, from whom it passed to Ricahrd Slater in 1677. His daughter and co-heiress brought it to George Pole, whose grand-daughter married Sir Charles Sedley, 2nd Bt and MP (1721–78). Starting in 1754, Thomas Wright designed and oversaw the building of a new house, closely following Andrea Palladio's Villa Rotonda, near Vicenze, in Italy, which

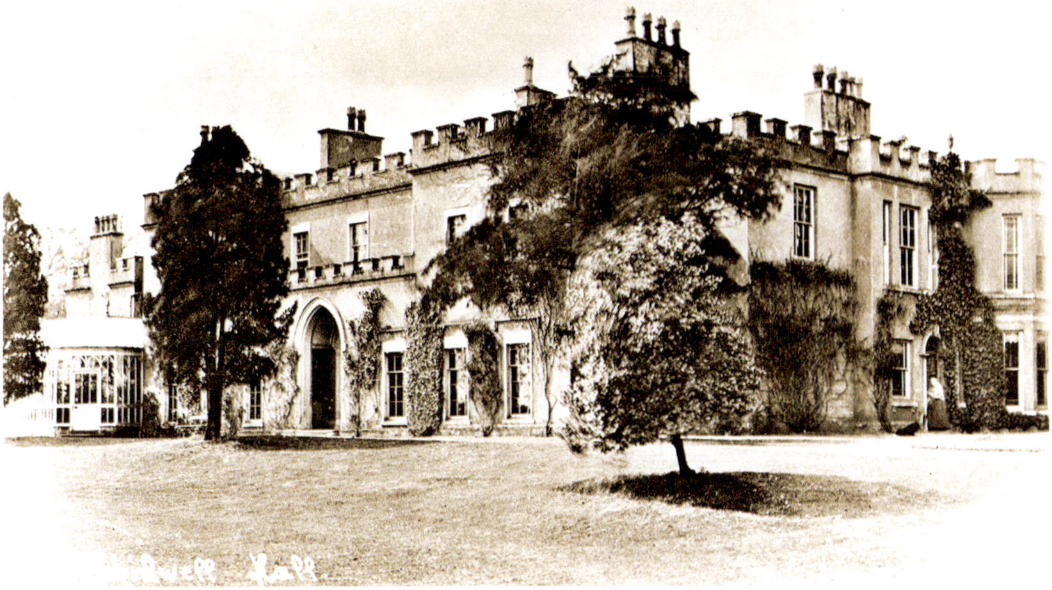

Chilwell Hall, from the south-east, *c.* 1899. From a postcard. (James Darwin)

had already been the direct inspiration for Lord Burlington's Chiswick (1725–29), his pupil Colen Campbell's Mereworth (1723–27) and nearby Foots Cray (by another Burlington follower, Isaac Ware, 1753–57), the last two being in Sir Charles's native Kent. Unlike the two Kentish houses, which followed Palladio's four-porticoed fronts, Nuthall had a single portico in antis, plain sides, and a top-lit dome over an octagonal gallery with ironwork by Benjamin Yates of Derby after Robert Bakewell, with Rococo stucco decoration by Thomas Roberts of Oxford. The west front was rebuilt with a pediment enclosing a Serliana over a canted bay in 1778–79 for Hon. Henry Vernon (later Sedley), husband of Sedley's heiress, and possibly the work of Joseph Pickford of Derby working in conjunction with William Emes, who re-landscaped the setting. James Wyatt made internal alterations a generation later. The Vernons sold in 1819 to Robert Holden of Darley Abbey (Derbyshire), the last of whom died at Nuthall in 1926. No buyer being found, this architecturally important house was demolished in 1929 bar the ruined central core, which survived until bulldozed for the M1 extension in 1966.

39. Arno Vale House, Arnold, Nottingham, 1935

Arno Vale began as a Regency villa of two and a half storeys with a four-bay garden front centered on paired tripartite fenestration. It is not clear for whom it was built, although Revd Mr Biddle was an occupier fairly early on, but by 1850 it was the property of Charles Sneath, whose heirs sold a decade or so later to lace thread spinner John Lawson Thackeray (d. 1886). He decided to transform the unpretentious house into a miniature French château, replacing

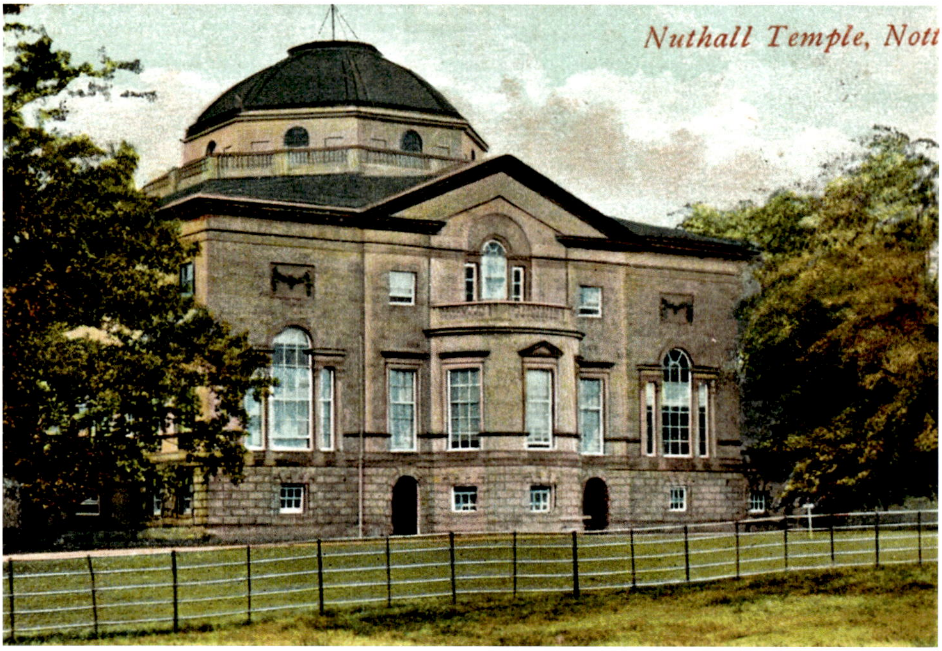

Nuthall Temple east front, as altered in the 1770s. From a chromolithographic postcard. (M. Craven)

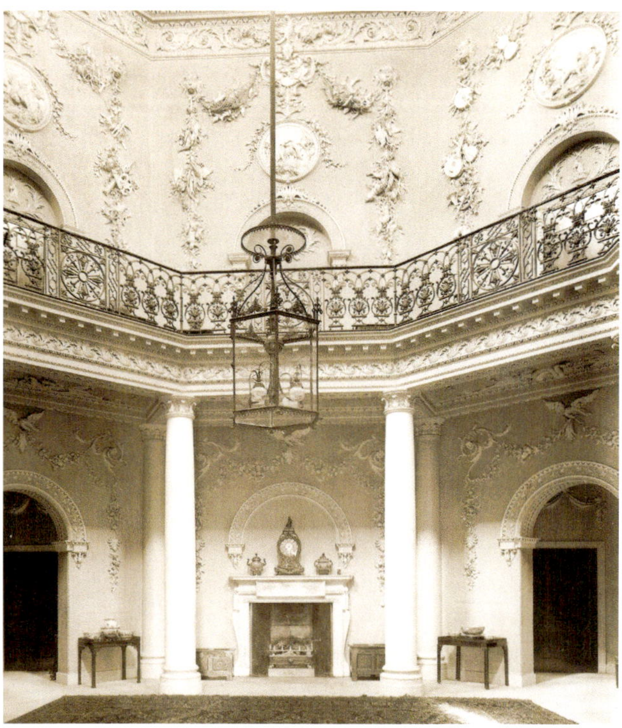

Nuthall Temple's top-lit octagonal central hall, showing Thomas Roberts' rococo plasterwork and Benjamin Yates' wrought-iron balustrade. (NMR)

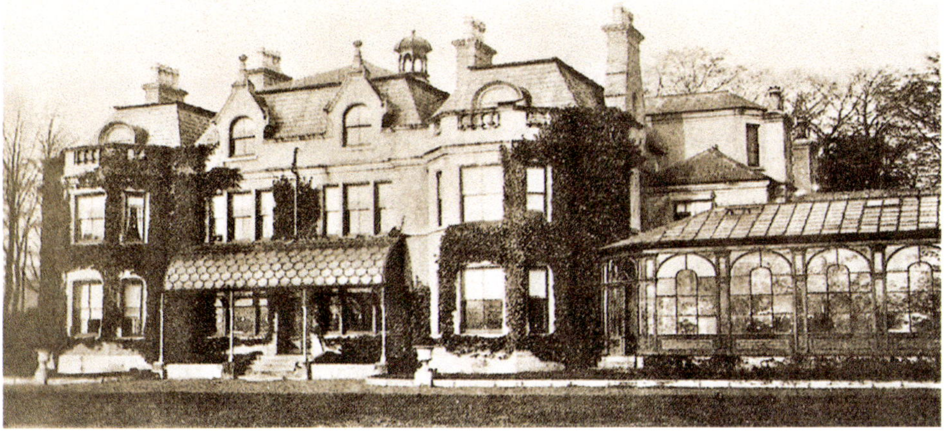

Arno Vale south front as rebuilt. From a postcard. (Bamfords Ltd)

the attic storey with arched and gabled dormers projecting from a triple-hipped roof originally adorned with iron brattishing and a miniature cupola. The end bays were rebuilt as canted projections with a fish-scale roofed verandah between. The architect was probably Robert Evans (1811–82), formerly the partner of T. C. Hine. The original service wing remained, shielded from view by a Messenger & Co. conservatory. In the early twentieth century, the house was let to the misses Fisher, members of another lace-making dynasty, before demolition came in summer 1935, a victim of the inexorable expansion of Nottingham.

40. Elton Manor, Elton-on-the-Hill (Gatepiers, II), 1935

The estate at Elton, secularised at the Reformation to the Yorkes, descended to the grand Nottingham family of Collin, whose heiress, Elizabeth, married Cornelius Launder. In 1806 a later Cornelius died, having built a neat two-storey five-bay Georgian house. He left the estate to his elder daughter, married in 1807 to William Norton (1781–1866), natural son of 2nd Lord Grantley, who doubled the house in size, rendering it and adding ramped parapets. On his death, the estate passed to her sister's son, William, 4th Count Randon de Pully (1821–92), on whose death the house and estate were purchased by Norton's nephew, John, 5th Lord Grantley, who like his predecessor used the house only occasionally as a shooting box, reducing the house accordingly. He sold in 1930 to a local man who let it to Sir Henry Readett-Bayley KBE (1878–1940), who moved out in 1933 (taking the main entrance gates with him) and it was again sold to W. N. Parr, who demolished it two years later. Two surviving listed eighteenth-century rusticated gate piers with iron gates remain on-site.

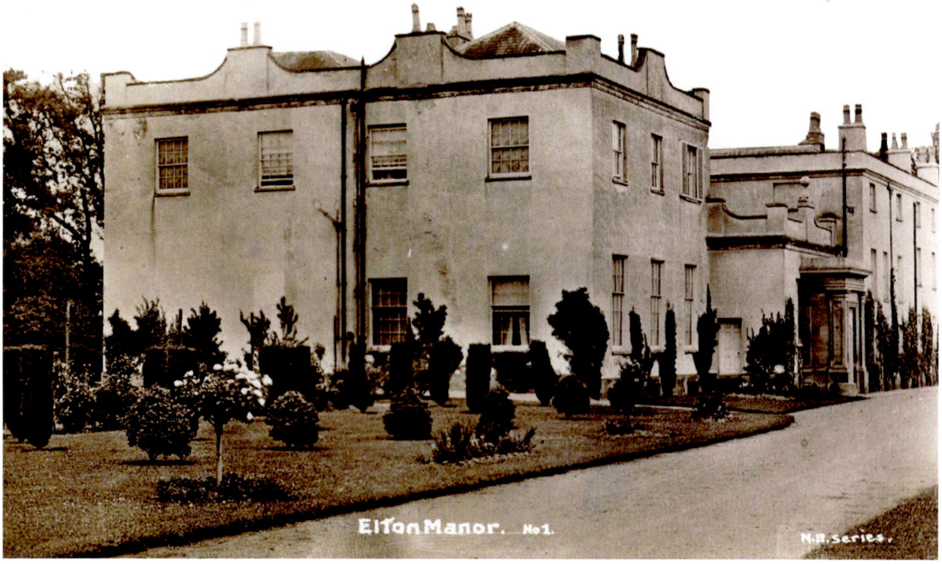

Elton Manor entrance front. From a postcard. (James Darwin)

41. Stapleford Hall, 1937

The Tevery family acquired the Stapleford estate from the de Staplefords. The last of the line, Sir Gervase Tevery, built a new three-storey house but died in 1639, his daughter and heiress bringing it to her husband, George Ashby of Quenby Hall (Leicsestershire). In 1675 it was all sold to Arthur Warren. The house was re-fronted by his descendant Admiral Sir John Borlase Warren 1st Bt MP (d. 1825) in 1797. It was of two storeys and nine bays (three central bays being recessed and with Serlian windows (later altered to lancets, probably during alterations by William Patterson, in around 1836) sill bands, stuccoed and with an ornamental parapet strongly suggesting the same architect as Elton Manor (see No. 40, p. 47). In 1839 the estate passed in trust to Sir John's great-grandson, Hon. William Vernon, second son of 5th Lord Vernon. When he came of age in 1855, he let it to Nottingham banker and scholar Ichabod Charles Wright (d. 1871, see No. 68 Bramcote Hills and No. 75 Lamcote House), who later bought the freehold and added a vast conservatory to the garden front. In 1893 it was sold to Mrs Margaret Elmore, who in 1901 sold to Nottingham property developer Sir Albert Ball, who (inevitably) sold the estate for housing and the timber. The house and the remaining 2 acres was sold to Frank Towle, followed by Richard Burrows, whose son, William, demolished it in 1937.

42. Broxtowe Hall, 1937

Broxtowe Hall was built in the second decade of the seventeenth century by Thomas Smith, a son of Sir Francis Smith of Ashby Folville (Leicestershire), who had purchased it from the Willoughbys of Wollaton under whom the previous house had been let to the Helwys family. It was of two storeys, brick with stone

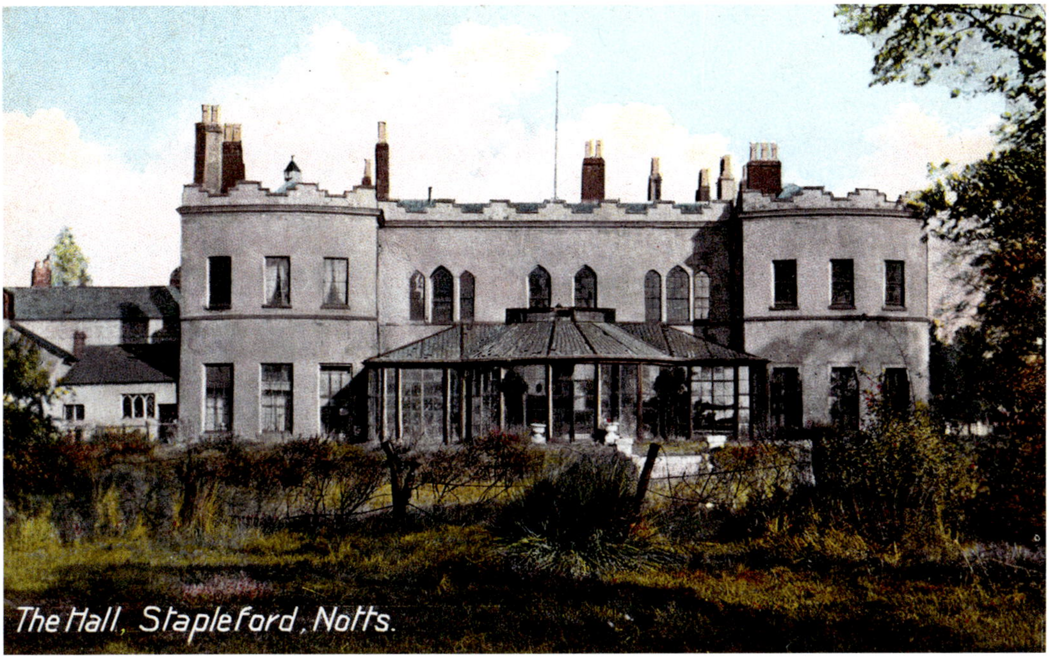

Stapleford Hall south (garden) front. From a colour-printed postcard. (James Darwin)

dressings and with a flat parapeted roof over the five bay central section, set off by a full-height portico, all flanked by cross-wings, probably relics of a previous house. Sir John Smith, after Civil War damage, replaced one cross-wing adorning it with shaped, almost Dutch, gables and mullioned and transom windows, but soon afterwards sold the estate to the Duke of Newcastle, under whom it was tenanted. In 1765, the 1st Duke (of the fourth creation) sold the 300-acre estate and house back to the Willoughbys in the person of 4th Lord Middleton. They immediately lowered the roof, adding a Serlian window to the entrance front to adapt it as a farmhouse, and in the mid-nineteenth century a balustraded square bay was added below the Serliana, with the cross-wing gable ends rebuilt in matching style embellished by ornamental bargeboards. Joseph Shepperson 'farmer and maltster' was the Wollaton estate tenant from *c.* 1831, and in 1864 his widow was in occupation. The house and grounds were subject of a Nottingham CPO and, in spring 1937, the house was sacrificed to make way for an estate of municipal housing.

43. Bulwell Wood Hall, Hucknall Torkard, 1937

John Throsby, writing in 1796 remarked, 'Bullwell Wood Hall, without the village, is inhabited by a farmer of the name of Freeman', thus emphasising that this house was only ever a secondary seat, originally of the Byrons of Newstead, to whom it came with the dissolution of Newstead Priory. Before 1579 it was used as the seat of the son and heir of Sir John Byron and a reused datestone of 1584 might suggest a rebuilding by them, although the evidence suggests that the house was

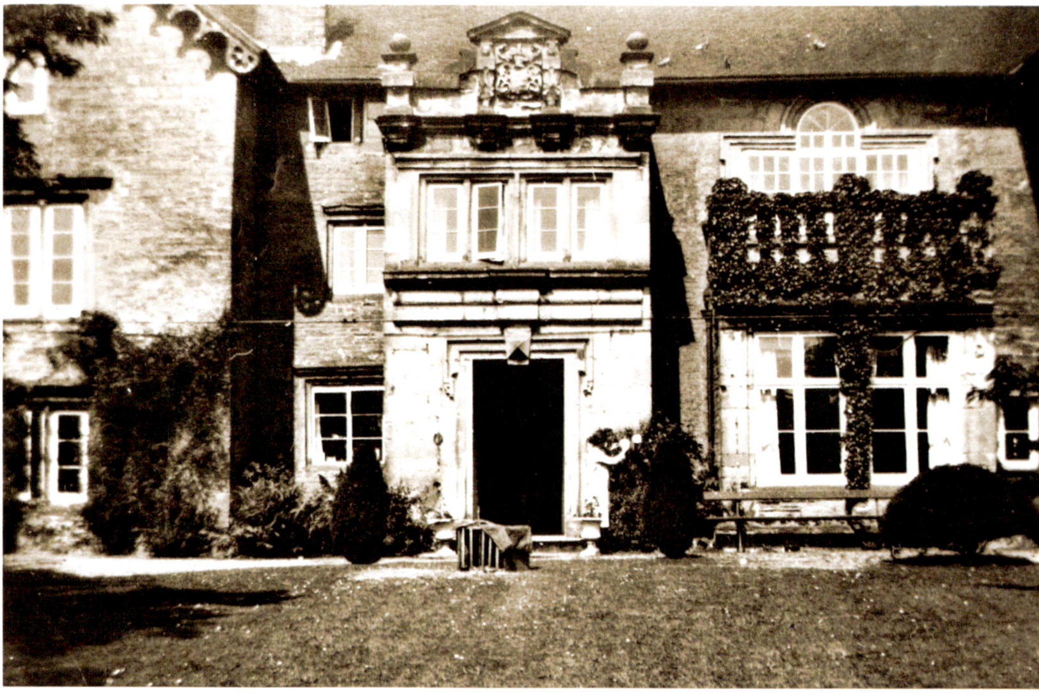

Broxtowe Hall's two-storey portico, 1920s. (Late Maurice Brassington)

demolished around 1630. It was replaced in brick with stone dressings by 1657 for Hon. William Byron was in residence prior his to succeeding as 3rd Lord Byron in 1679; he paid tax on fourteen hearths in 1674. The new house was very up to date for its period, having a classical south front under a plain tiled roof of seven bays, with stone cross windows and an offset entrance via a muscular pedimented stone doorcase with a Vanburgh-like keyblock, although there was a vernacular gable wing behind of two storeys with attics, earlier mullioned windows and a stair tower containing an oak newel stair, presumably retained from the previous house. When the 3rd Lord Byron succeeded the house was occupied by the Truman family, remaining there for many generations (suffering a fire in 1758), although in the Regency period the Newstead estate sold the property as a working farm to the Duke of Portland as part of a land rationalisation. The Welbeck estate changed the fenestration for sashes, but later in the nineteenth century the ground-floor windows were replaced with multi-light mullioned and transomed ones. The estate sold it in the later 1920s. By the early 1930s there were no tenants and the house was in decay. Inevitably, it was burnt out, probably through unauthorised occupation, in May 1937, although the shell remained in situ until 1953.

44. Clumber Park (I, II* and II), 1938

After the 1870 fire Clumber was replaced in somewhat ponderous style by Charles Barry, junior, to no good aesthetic effect. Although the two-storey corner pavilions on the south-east front were kept, the main body of the new building

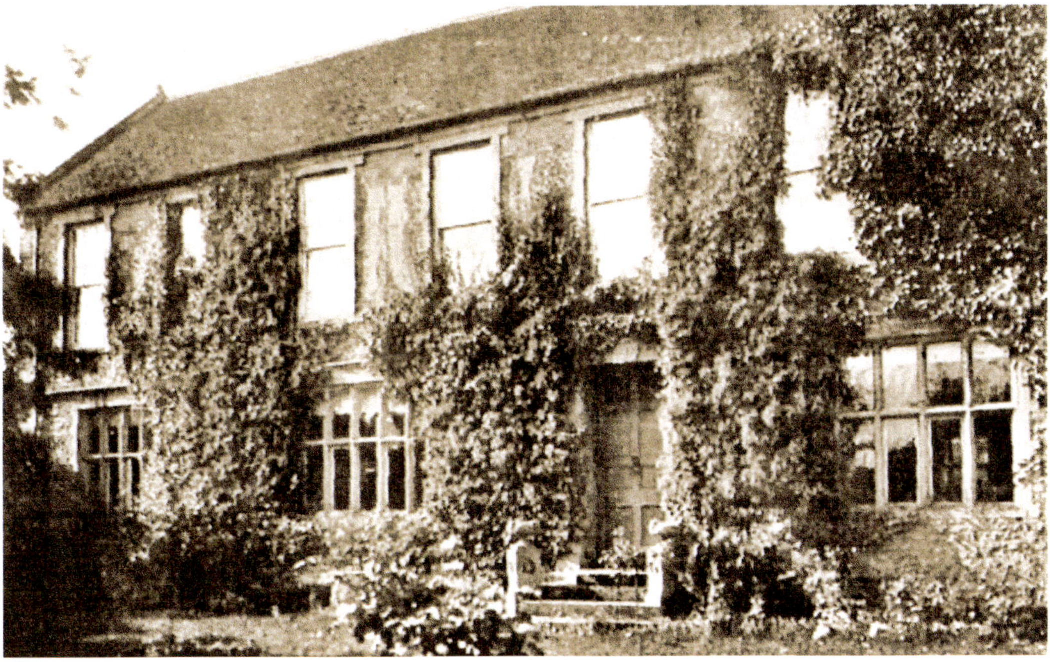

Bulwell Wood Hall entrance front. (Thoroton Society)

was lower, of only two storeys, with the blind arcading of the pavilions extended as a loggia of paired columns between the two. The north-east front was extended to twelve bays, acquiring a pair of three-storey towers with rather Teutonic-looking tops in the central breakfront, which were later removed. The interior was replaced on a lavish scale with an emphasis on ornament. The 7th Duke also commissioned the unforgettably striking church from G. F. Bodley in 1880–89. In 1912, yet another fire damaged the north-west (service) wing. Restoration was undertaken, but on the death of the duke in 1928 the family gave up on it, selling parts of the estate and the contents. In 1938 Charles Boot demolished the entire house, bar the study, stables and chapel, taking chimneypieces and garden statuary to his house at Thornbridge, Derbyshire, where they remain. The National Trust acquired the estate in 1945, opening it a year later using the stable block as their regional HQ. The footprint of the house now picked out on the ground.

45. Nettleworth Hall, 1940

Located to the south of Sookholme, Nettleworth Hall was the centrepiece of the estate and was built in 1566 by William Wylde, but little is known of its appearance except that it was of local stone. The hall was rebuilt following a fire in 1785 as a two-and-a-half-storey, three-bay villa. It was sold by the Wylde family to Henry Gally Knight FRS (1786–1846), who had married Selina, sister of Alleyne FitzHerbert, Lord St Helens, from whose posterity it passed to Sir Henry FitzHerbert, 3rd Bt of Tissington, Derbyshire. Sir William, 4th Bt,

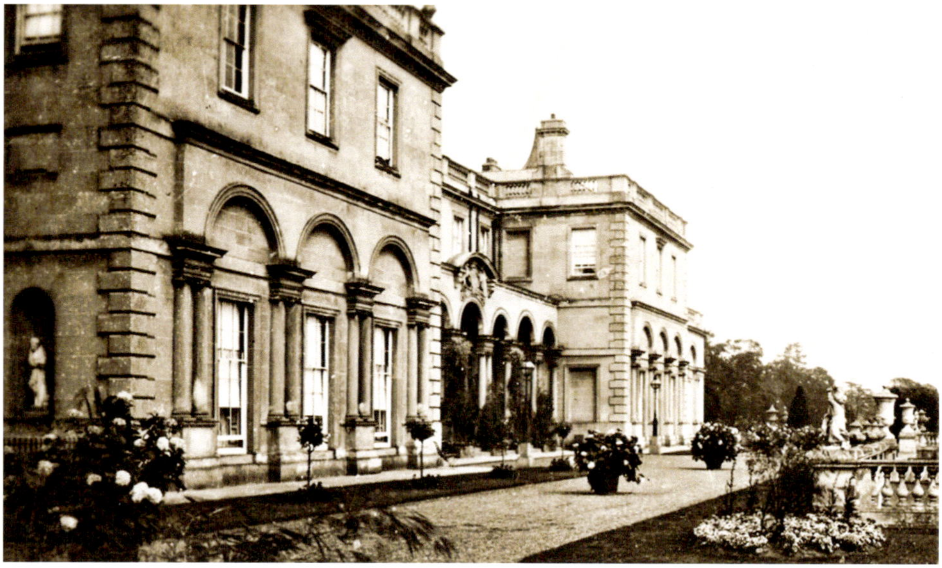

Clumber Park (II), the front of the virtually new house, *c.* 1904. View from the east and from a postcard sent 1908. (M. Craven)

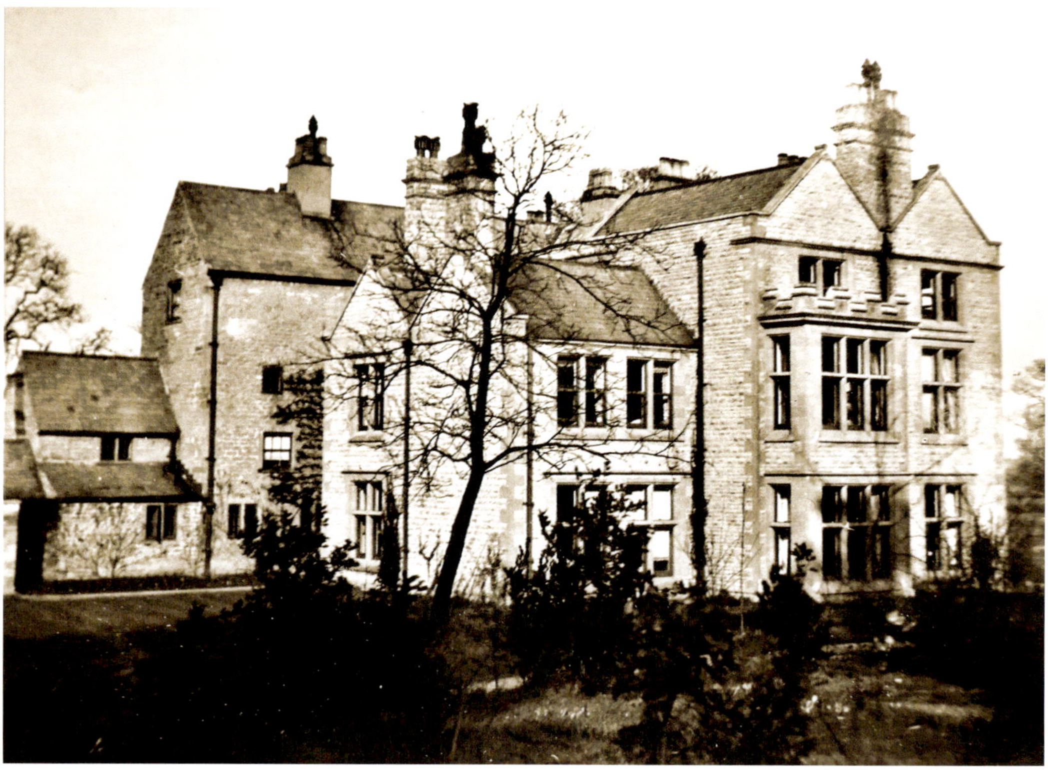

Nettleworth Hall south front, *c.* 1894. (Sir Richard FitzHerbert, Bt)

undertook a thoroughgoing rebuilding, adding a gabled south-west wing, canted bays, and mullion and transom fenestration. When Revd Sir Richard Fitzherbert inherited the baronetcy in 1896, he resigned as rector of Warsop and moved to Nettleworth. The house was eventually sold to the Nevilles, but not the estate, which the FitzHerberts have retained. In 1940 the Nevilles decided to dismantle the house to prevent the military commandeering it. Some walling and part of the service wing was left standing on-site, which has since been converted to residential use.

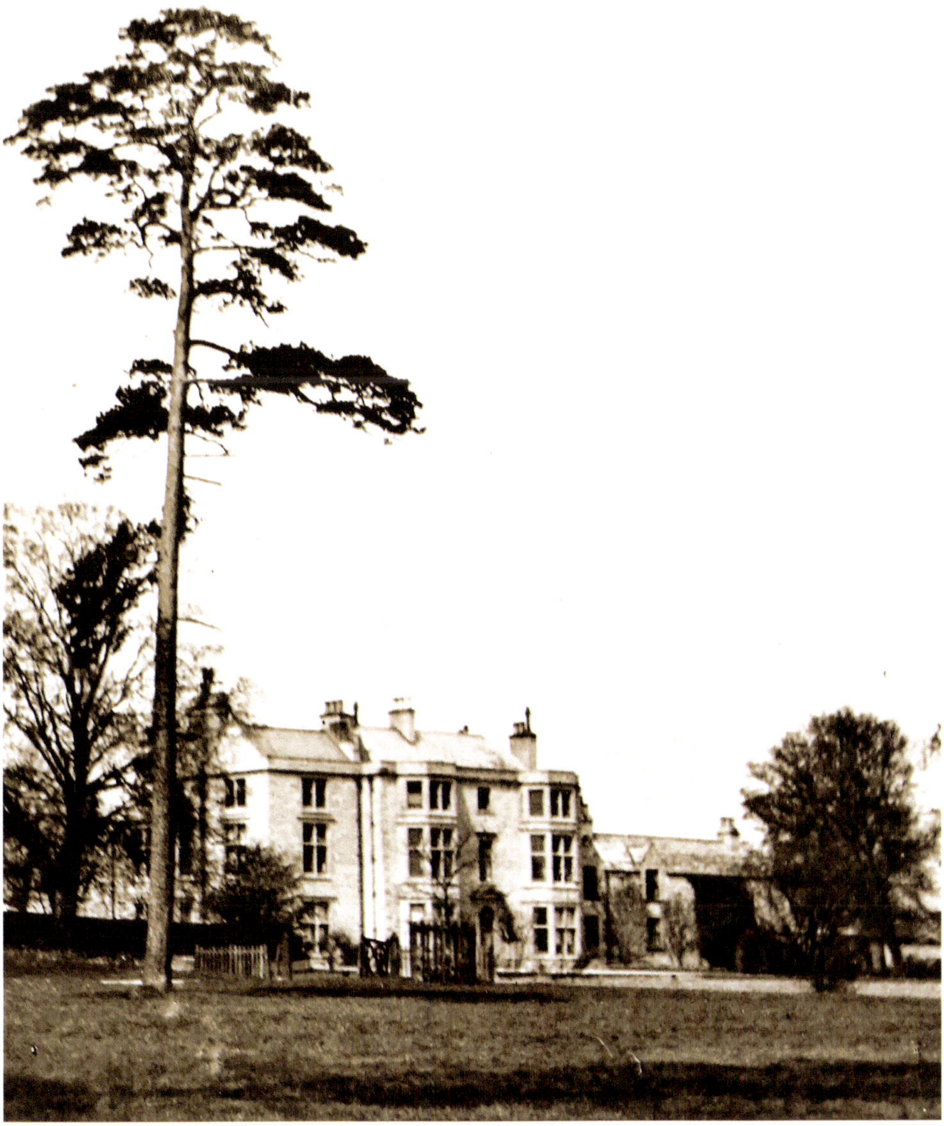

Nettleworth Hall entrance front, east, *c.* 1894. (Sir Richard FitzHerbert, Bt)

Section Five

Losses Since 1945

46. Morton Hall, Ranby, 1946

The manorial estate at Morton descended from Roger de Busli to the Vavasours of Shipley (Derbyshire), but by 1331 had passed to the Strelleys of Strelley, fragmenting later, and no known capital mansion had stood within the estate. In 1746, a major portion of the estate was bought by George Mason (1708–74), son of a rector of Ordsall and grandson of Paul Mason of Eaton, a village not far south-east of Morton, where the family remained until George William Mason JP DL (1819–91), third in descent from George, commissioned James Fowler of Louth, Lincolnshire (a church and schools specialist), to build him a seat of some pretention. Built between 1865 and 1869, Morton Hall was Jacobethan, of two storeys, brick with stone dressings, with a *porte cochère*, profusion of gables replete with finials and kneelers, mullioned and transomed windows and an ogiform tower, making a moderately arresting ensemble. W. H. Mason (1846–1936), an advocate with a penchant for painting, depicted the house as shown here in watercolour, but his grandson, the diplomat Sir Paul Mason KCMG

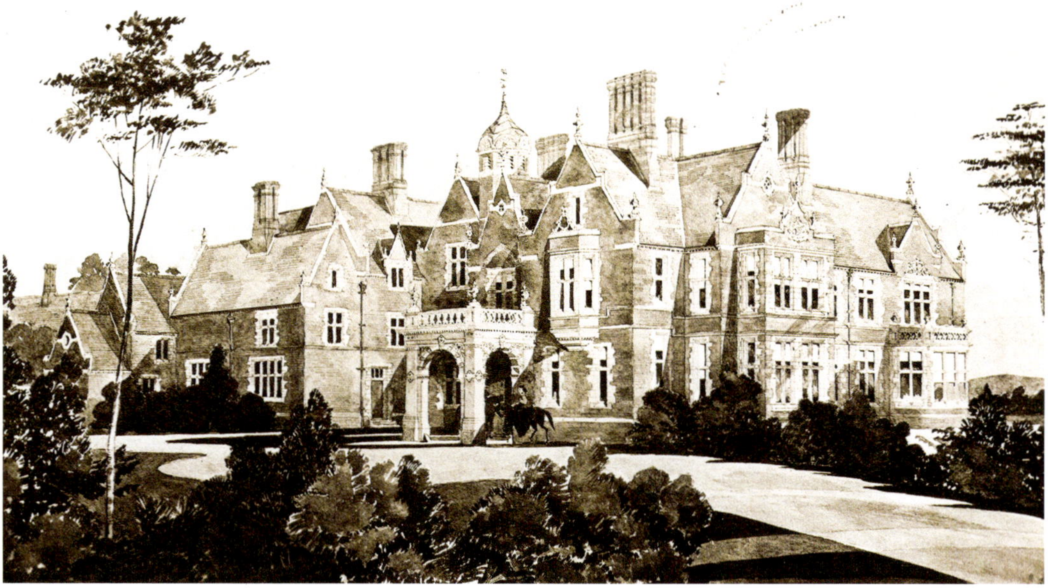

Morton Hall, Ranby. Painting by W. H. Mason in the mid-nineteenth century. (James Darwin)

(1904–78) demolished it in 1946 due to damage caused by wartime military occupation, building a new more modest dwelling adjacent.

47. Rampton Manor, *c.* 1946

After more than a century without a seat at Rampton (see No. 11, p. 17), the Eyre family decided once again to build a house there. As a result, Revd Charles Wasteneys Eyre (1802–62), who inherited from his uncle Anthony in 1836, commissioned the prolific Scots country house architect William Burn to design the house, which was built 1851–53. The result was a four-square two-storey house with canted bays, a forest of tall chimneys, a shaped attic gable at the right end of teach front, except for the south-east angle where there was an ogee capped tower, seemingly the inspiration of that at Morton (see p. 52). Strangely, the fenestration was sashed throughout with glazing bars to the attic windows, below which was a prominent cornice supporting the parapet. There was a lower service wing to the east. The son, Colonel Henry Eyre CB (1834–1904), sold the house with 1,400 acres to John Andrew Cottam of The Priory, South Leverton (1855–1923), who in turn sold in 1902 to steel maker Sir Charles Ellis GBE KCB (1853–1937). He sold during the First World War in order to move to be near London where he served as Director General of Ordnance. After a succession of owners, it lay empty and was demolished shortly after the Second World War, leaving only the entrance arch to the estate, just west of the church, provided by Burn with cresting to echo the outline of the old gateway in the churchyard (see p. 17).

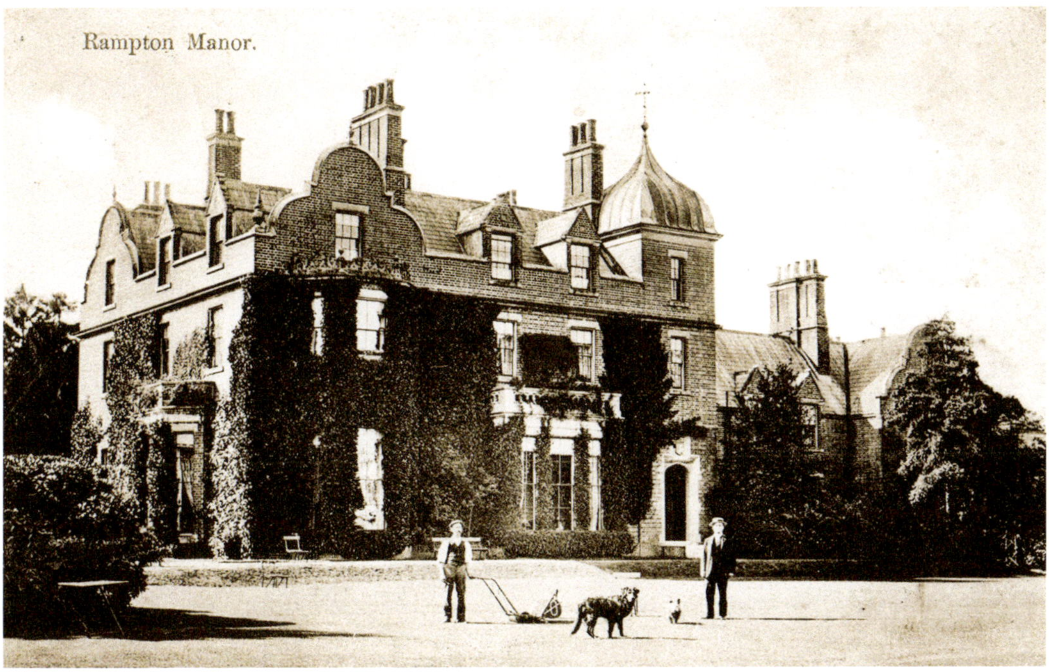

Rampton Manor. From a postcard. (James Darwin)

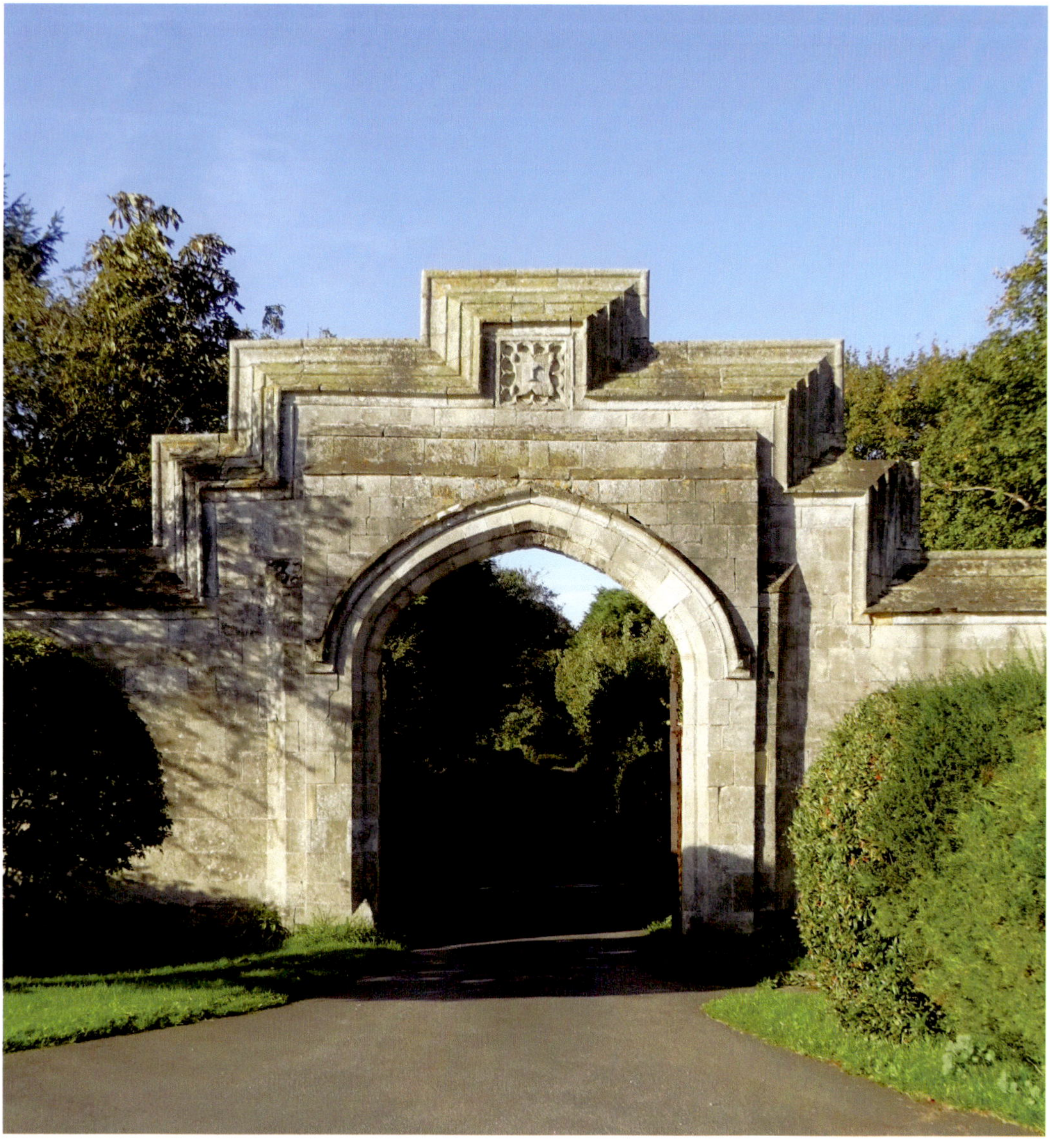

Rampton Manor's surviving entrance arch in the village, October 2023. (Carole Craven)

48. Grove Hall, 1951

There are undated drawings by Robert or John Smythson in the RIBA Smythson collection, which seem intended as designs for a replacement for an older house for Sir John Hercy, whose remote ancestor, Sir Malveysin de Hercy, had inherited Grove through marriage in the twelfth century. It is presumed that this was never built, and the estate soon afterwards passed by marriage to George Nevile of Thorney (see p. 77), whose descendant, Sir Edward Nevile, 1st Bt, died without an heir in 1686, when the eminent judge Sir Creswell Levinz (1627–1701) bought it, remodelling the ancient house. Anthony Eyre MP, son of Anthony of Rampton (see p. 55), who had died in 1748, bought it in 1762 from Sir Creswell's grandson and commissioned John Carr of York to entirely rebuild the house, endowing it with a relentlessly plain two-storey south front with a central canted bay, a new west entrance and staircase, the latter lit by a first-floor Serlian window. In 1790 William Lindley of Doncaster was called in to add lodges, while Humphrey Repton re-landscaped the 200-acre park and, in 1794, Lindley made alterations to the house, too, including rendering it in Roman cement. Anthony, uncle of Revd Charles Eyre of Rampton, left Grove to his daughter and co-heiress, the wife of Granville Harcourt Vernon JP, a son of Edward, Archbishop of York 1807–47 and a grandson of 1st Lord Vernon. His great-grandson Colonel Granville Harcourt Vernon DSO, OBE, MC, JP (1891–1974) sold the contents in 1932. The house and estate went to Canon R. F. Wilkinson, who sold up in 1946, when the government used the house temporarily to home families home from India after the partition, but this soon ended and the building was demolished bar the stable block and Lindley's lodges in 1951.

49. Carlton Hall, Carlton-in-Lindrick, 1955

Like Clumber and other seats in Sherwood Forest, Carlton Hall began as a hunting lodge built for the Clifton family in the early seventeenth century. The

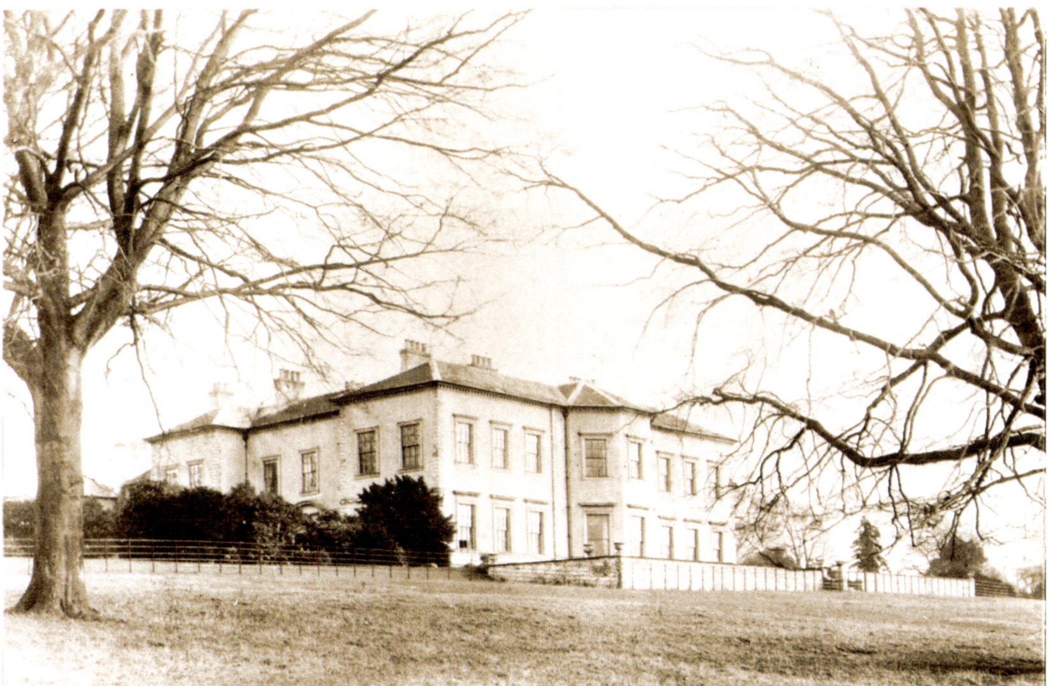

Grove from the south-west, *c.* 1890. From Cornelia, Lady Craven's house party album, 1908 (M. Craven)

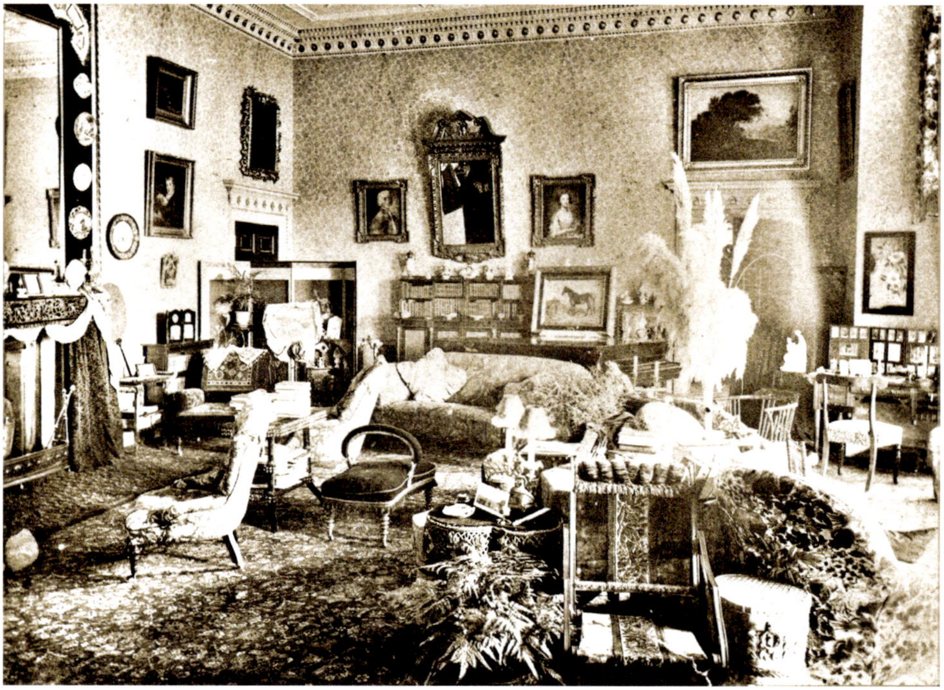

Grove drawing room, *c.* 1890. From Cornelia, Lady Craven's house party album, 1908 (M. Craven)

estate was sold to the Mellishes of Blyth in 1765. Our first record of the house is an enclosure map of 1769, which shows that it had a formal landscape setting, consisting of a wide lawn near the house and a 'wilderness' or woodland area with intersecting rides, many of which emanated from a *patte d'oie* near the house. This landscape is likely to have been an early eighteenth-century creation, and echoes the type of landscapes that were being created on hunting estates in France at the time, not to mention Haughton and Averham. Neither the Clifton nor the Mellish families ever lived at Carlton, so the house at this time was probably still relatively modest. In 1774 the estate was sold to Major Robert Ramsden, fourth son of Sir William, 2nd Bt of Byrom (1708–69). His son, another Robert (1753–1830), in 1783 brought in Derbyshire-based landscaper William Emes to remodel the setting. The lawns and woodland were replaced by sweeping parkland with a sinuous lake, much of which survives to the present. The house was rebuilt after Robert married the banker's widow, Mrs Abel Smith, in 1788. It was a plain-stuccoed seven-by-five-bay two-storey block under a hipped roof, the main (south) front having a three-bay pediment supported on pilaster strips with almost two-dimensional Ionic capitals and a nominal entablature, with a Doric porch below. The interior boasted neo-classical plasterwork, there was a fine top-lit staircase and a Regency iron verandah was later added to the west front. The Ramsdens moved to Wigthorpe Hall in 1871 and Carlton Hall was let. It was unoccupied by the 1920s and remained as such until it was requisitioned for use by a tank

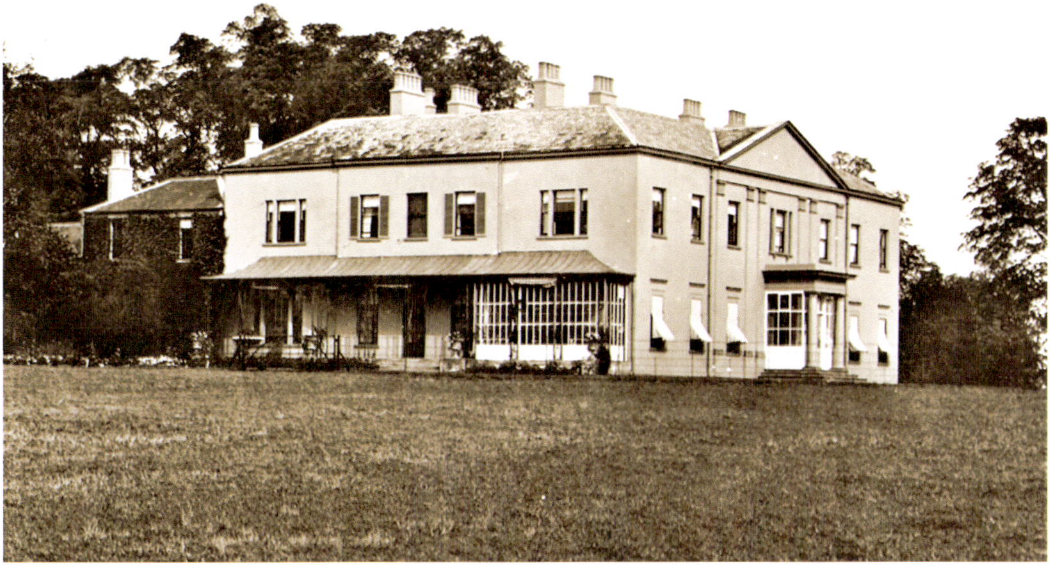

Carlton Hall, Carlton-in-Lindrick, seen from the south-west. From a postcard. (M. Craven)

regiment. Later in the Second World War the grounds housed Italian and German prisoners of war. The house was demolished in 1955 shortly after the military left the site, although its lodge, the majority of its outbuildings (known collectively as Carlton Hall Farm) survived. Two parts of the hall were reused elsewhere in the village: an iron veranda was attached to a bungalow on Long Lane and an archway was also earlier transferred to the gardens of Wigthorpe Hall.

50. Rufford Abbey, 1956

Rufford was the great seat of the 1st Marquess of Halifax and of four earls of Scarborough, essentially a house of William and Mary date but still in Carolean style, which was peremptorily demolished by Nottinghamshire County Council shortly after having been acquired with much of the estate in 1956. All that remains is an attenuated remnant of the early seventeenth-century house of the earls of Shrewsbury, resting on the remains of the Cistercian monastery founded in 1146 by Gilbert de Gant. The earls of Shrewsbury were the beneficiaries of the dissolution of the abbey, but this was *not* one of the houses Bess of Hardwick, the next countess, built. The surviving seventeenth-century gabled portion (very similar to Selston Hall, see p. 31) was the work of the 7th Earl. When the 8th Earl died in 1617, Rufford passed to his sister's husband, Yorkshire baronet Sir George Savile, whose descendant was Charles II's wily Lord Privy Seal, created Marquess of Halifax ('the Trimmer') in 1679. The vast expansion of the house, approximately following the H plan of its predecessor, may well have been the work of his friend Lord Craven's architect William Winde, certainly assisted by Charles Renny. It was of seven by nine by eight bays, of three storeys and

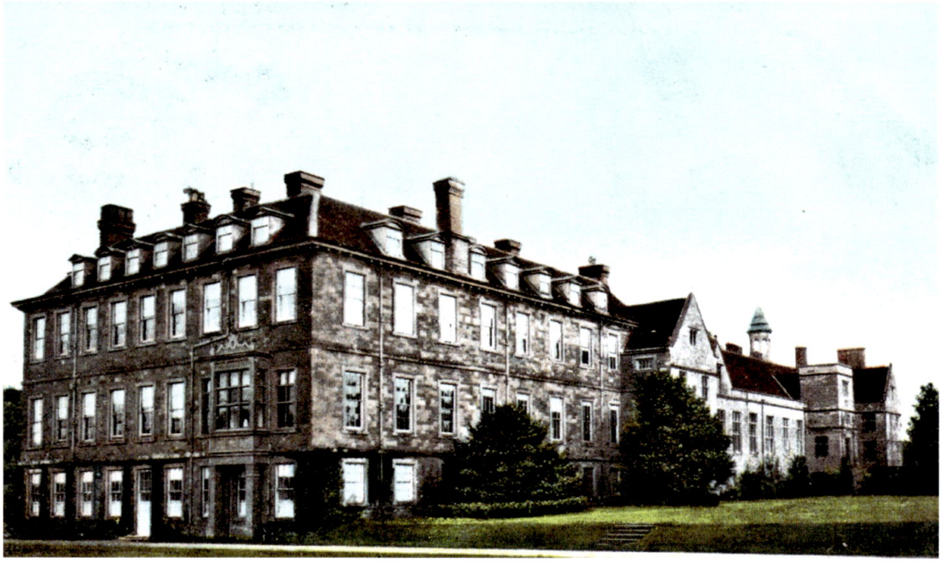

Rufford from the south-west. From a chromolithographic postcard sent in 1906. (M. Craven)

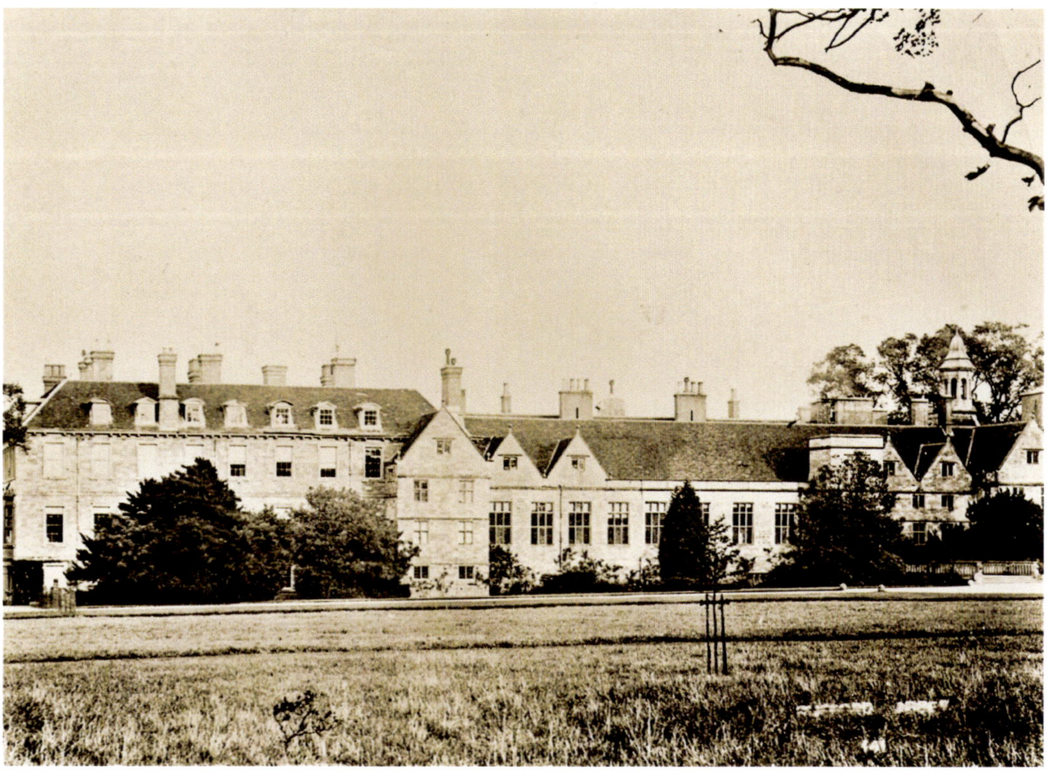

Rufford south front. 'Photographed with my Brownie' by Cornelia, Lady Craven, 1907. (M. Craven)

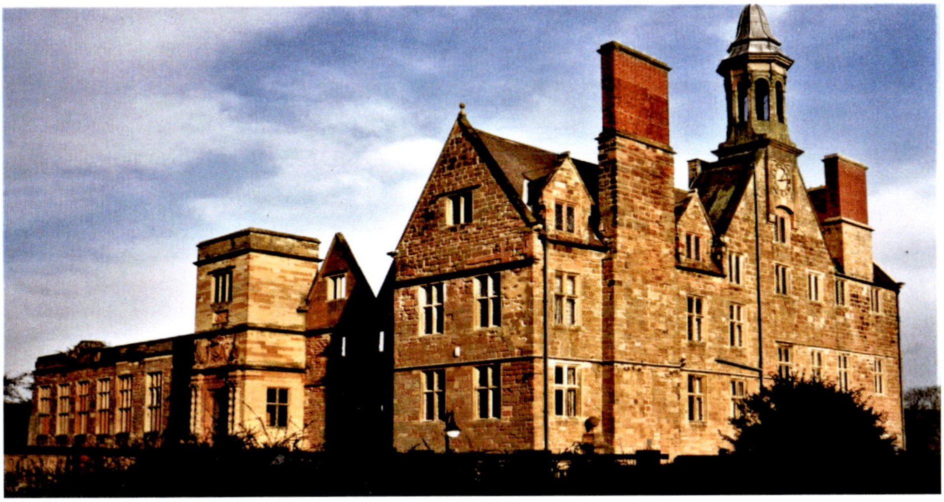

Rufford's surviving mainly seventeenth-century portion, 2002. (M. Craven)

attics, under hipped sprocketed roofs, with modest eared window surrounds. After the 2nd Lord Halifax's death in 1700, it all passed to a cousin, whose son, Sir George Savile, 7th Bt., FRS MP. beautified the park and created the surviving Bath Summer House in 1729. The last baronet died in 1784 when the estate passed to 5th Earl of Scarborough. The 8th Earl had Anthony Salvin primp the house in 1838–40 (he added the tall cupola to the Jacobean portion), but on the death of the 8th Earl in 1856, it passed to the diplomat John Lumley, a natural son, who was in 1888 created Lord Savile of Rufford. His heirs retreated to Yorkshire in 1938, and the deleterious effects of army occupation in the war encouraged the county council to demolish much of the house in 1956 – a great loss.

51. Wiseton Hall, 1956

Wiseton's early history was one of fragmented holdings, a situation which continued until the Civil War, by which time Thomas Wawyn held it, from whom it came by marriage to Robert Nelthorpe, scion of a Yorkshire family and MP for Beverley. It was also at Beverley that lived his cousins the Acklom family (originally of Moreby), of whom Jonathan (1651–1738) inherited the estate on the execution of Richard Nelthorpe for complicity in Monmouth's rebellion in 1685. His nephew Richard rebuilt the old house piecemeal (if Throsby is to be believed) ending up with a modest three-storey five bay-house completed in 1771 to deigns either by his prolific American cousin Philip Harrison, or by William Lindley, who was certainly called in to add Palladian wings and a stable block in 1787. The heiress brought the estate to 3rd Earl Spencer, but died in childbirth, leading to the estate being sold on Lord Spencer's death in 1845 to Revd Christopher Neville of Thorney (who let it to another parson, Robert Manners Sutton). It was sold again in 1863 to Durham-based magnate Joseph Laycock for his son, Robert Laycock MP, who greatly extended it to the east adding a lower tower and to the west a sumptuous dining room.

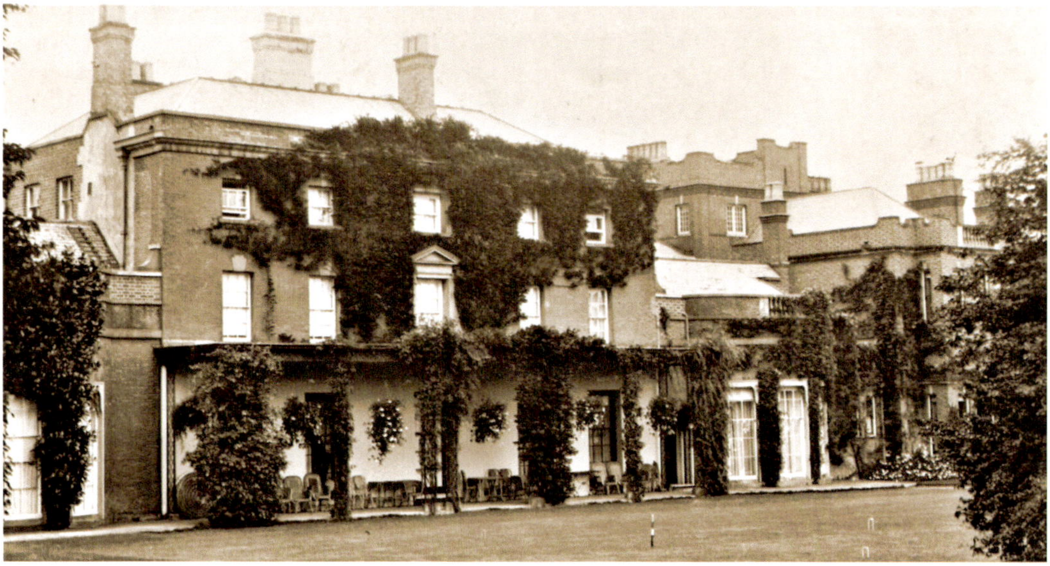

Wiseton Hall's eighteenth-century garden front with Victorian additions crowding it from the right. From a postcard sent in 1908. (M. Craven)

John Oldrid Scott 'beautified' Clayworth church in 18740–75 at Robert Laycock's expense, so it is possible he designed the additions to the hall, too. Brigadier Sir Joseph Laycock, KCMG, DSO, TD, JP (d. 1952) made further alterations in 1904 and rebuilt the stables, but his son, Major General Sir Robert Laycock, KCMG, CB, DSO was governor and commander in chief in Malta when he decided to demolish the house as it was too big. On his return in 1959 he set about replacing it with a more modest house, albeit still in restrained Georgian taste, sold by the family in 1992.

52. Cockglode Hall, Edwinstowe, 1957

The Hay of Bilhaugh and Birklands was long a portion of the Forest of Sherwood held by the Crown and under the supervision of a ranger whose lodge stood on the side of Bilhaugh Hill, a building much neglected by Queen Anne's reign when it was described 'a tumbledown cottage'. The house recorded as having been built there on land leased in 1724 by William Sterne, may have been on a different site, as contemporary maps show the *patte d'oie* well to the north of the Cockglode House built by Dr George Aldridge who had obtained a new Crown lease in 1776. The house, built 1776–77, was really a villa set in a wooded glade, with central canted bays in the manner of John Carr on the east and west fronts with superimposed Serlian windows much in the manner of Joseph Pocklington on the returns which ended in gables, whereas the remaining roofs were hipped. On Aldridge's death in 1797 the lease passed to Sir Robert Shore Milnes Bt and then to Colonel Savile Lumley, son of the 4th Earl of Scarborough of Rufford. However, in 1828 the Crown exchanged the Hay for a preferment held by the Duke of Portland, who in turn exchanged it with Earl Manvers in 1833, making

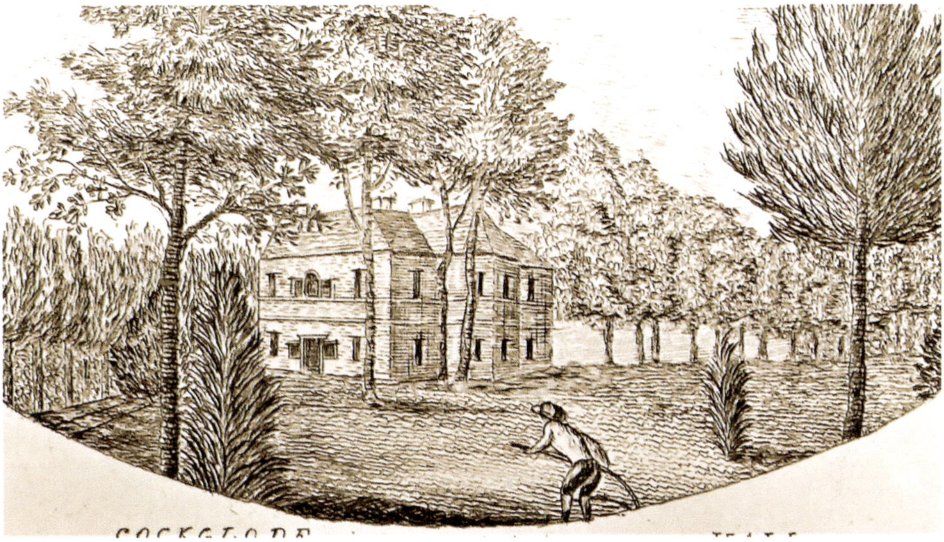

Cockglode Hall, as depicted by Throsby, 1796. (M. Craven)

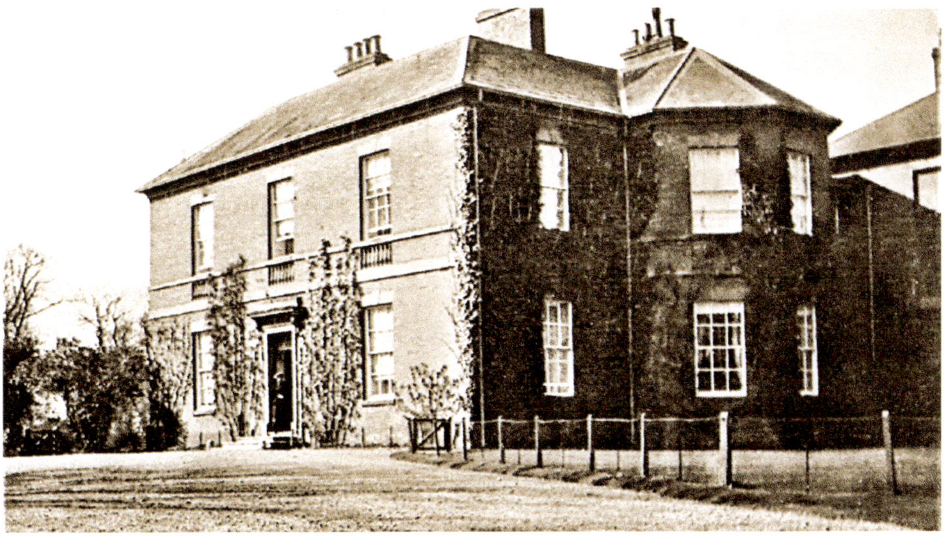

Cockglode Hall from the south-west, as rebuilt, in the 1920s. (Private collection)

it part of the Thoresby estate, although the Lumleys' lease was not surrendered until 1869, when a new one was granted to the Foljambes of Osberton, making Cockglode a secondary residence on the estate. It was occupied for many years by Cecil Foljambe MP (1846–1907), later 1st Earl of Liverpool, for whom the house was greatly extended to the west and north in plain, almost Regency style in 1884. Lord Liverpool's nephew George succeeded him but in 1912, it was let to widow Eva, Mrs George Hutton *née* Brooke, previously wife of Hon. Cornwallis Maude, only son of the 1st (and last) Earl of Montalt and her daughter Eveline.

Mrs Hutton died in 1940, her daughter moved away to Thoresby and the house was divided into eight flats until 1955 when the estate required the site to dump spoil from a new deep pit at Thoresby Colliery, and the house was accordingly demolished in 1956.

53. Oxton Hall, 1957

Oxton was divided between three manorial estates, and ownership there remained fragmented for centuries. The Strelleys held one part and another was held by the Saviles. The latter portion was purchased in 1571 from George Purefoy of Drayton, Leicestershire, by Thomas Sherbrook (anciently Shirebrook) formerly of Shirebrook in Derbyshire and his family held the estate there until 1957, and built the house shortly afterwards and it remained the chief seat of the family until 1779. Meanwhile, the Sherbrookes had died out in the male line in 1754, and there followed a series of successions by husbands and progeny of Henry Sherbrooke's three daughters but, by 1845, even their posterity had failed in the male line and the estate reverted to Henry Lowe (later Sherbrooke), great-grandson of Henry Sherbrooke's sister. However, in 1779 William Sherbrooke, son of William Coape – builder of Sherwood Lodge (see No. 73, p. 88) – landscaped the park (to include a lake – perhaps Emes again?) and built a new house of three storeys and seven bays, of execrable proportions, the breakfront consisting of a portico in antis and three very crowded bays set beneath a very wide thermal window topped by a pediment, surely the work of a local builder adapting very freely from a pattern book. If Throsby is to be believed, the old house, sited in what later became the kitchen garden, lingered on with a tenant until after about

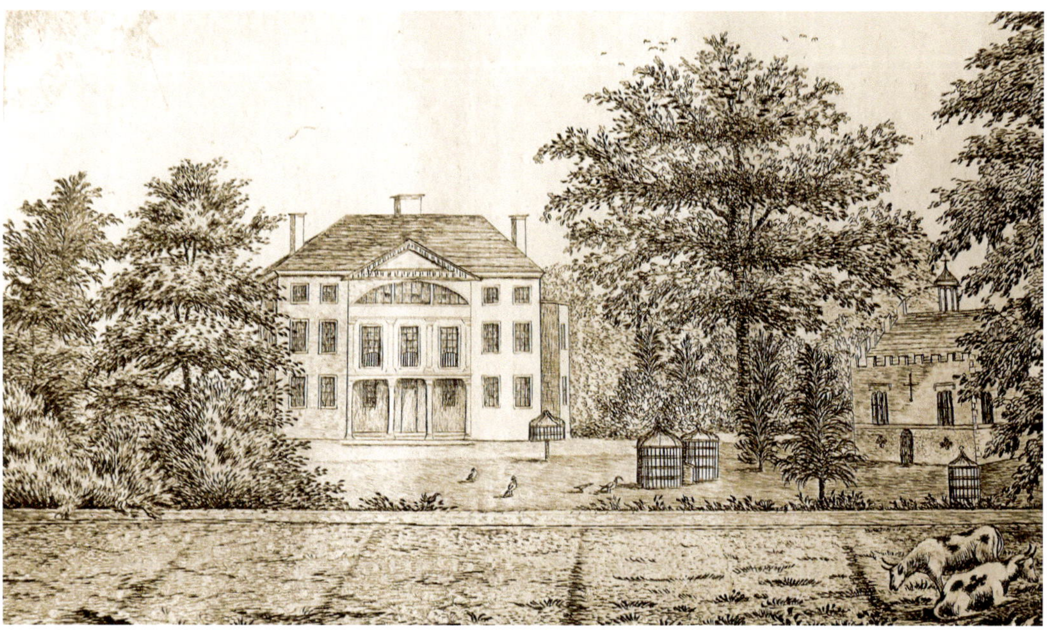

Oxton Hall's south front, as depicted by Throsby, 1796. (M. Craven)

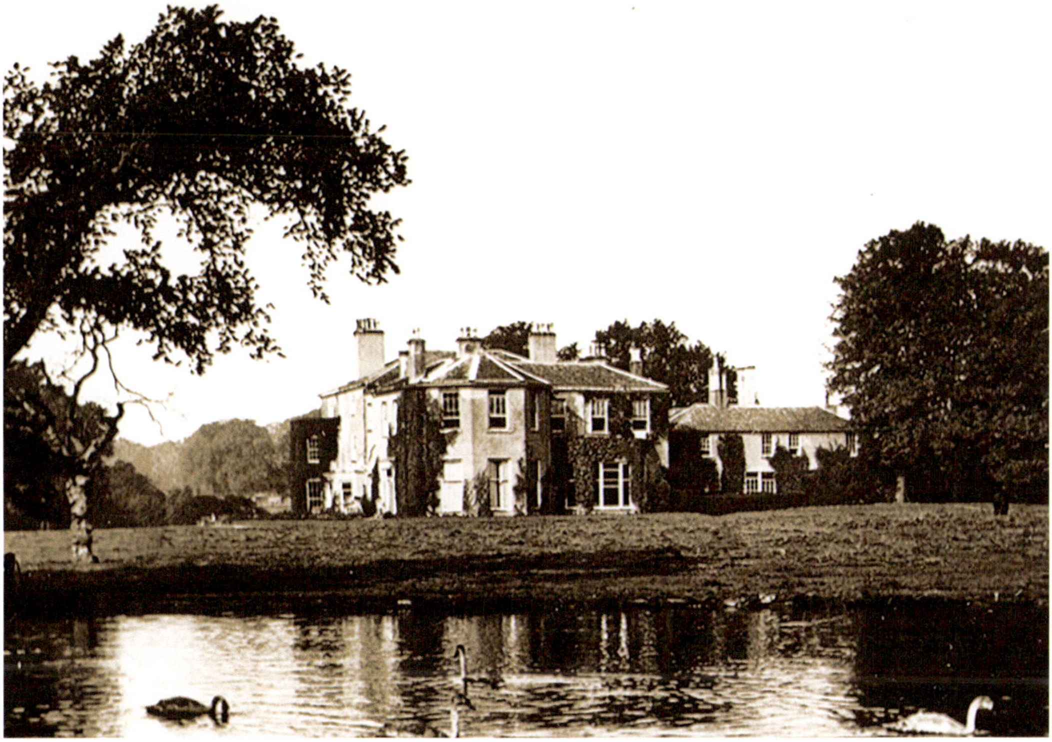

Oxton Hall from the lake, showing later additions. From a postcard. (James Darwin)

1800, but was soon afterwards demolished. Henry Sherbrooke (formerly Lowe) made a lower addition including two canted bays and a service wing, in 1847. The Sherbrooke family retained possession of the hall until 1957 when Rear Admiral Robert Sherbrooke VC, CB, DSO, DL (1901–72) demolished it, leaving only the Regency coach house and stable block.

54. Bulwell Hall, 1958

Bulwell had a complex history through the Medieval period, but was sold by the Crown in 1638 to Sir Edward Ayscough of South Kelsey, Lincolnshire, later passing to Sir Charles Sedley of Nuthall Temple. He later sold to returned West Indies merchant John Newton, who in 1770 built a well-proportioned five-bay, two-and-a-half-storey house entered through a tripartite door topped by a Serlian window below a top parapet, the whole being of brick with stone dressings. There were also two-storey single-bay wings linking to modest pavilions, in typical Palladian fashion. The house was locally referred to 'by himself and others', Throsby tells us, as Pye-wipe (Lapwing) Hall. The fact that Nottingham architect/builder William Roberts was estimating for alterations to the parish church in 1767 might suggest that he was designed and built Newton's House too. In 1827, Newton's heir, Godfrey Wentworth, sold the estate to Revd Alfred Padley, whose family held it until 1865 when the lordship, estate and advowson were purchased by Major Samuel Cooper JP (d. 1871), who added stables and coach house. Twelve years later, T. C. Hine was called in to extend the house for Percy Cooper. He enlarged the pavilions, extended the façade by three bays at each end, put in a clock tower behind with a domed roof, lantern and spirelet, unifying the whole ponderous ensemble with an urn-laden balustrade. In 1890 brewer Thomas Hardy acquired it, dying in 1897 and in 1908 his heirs sold it with 575 acres (and

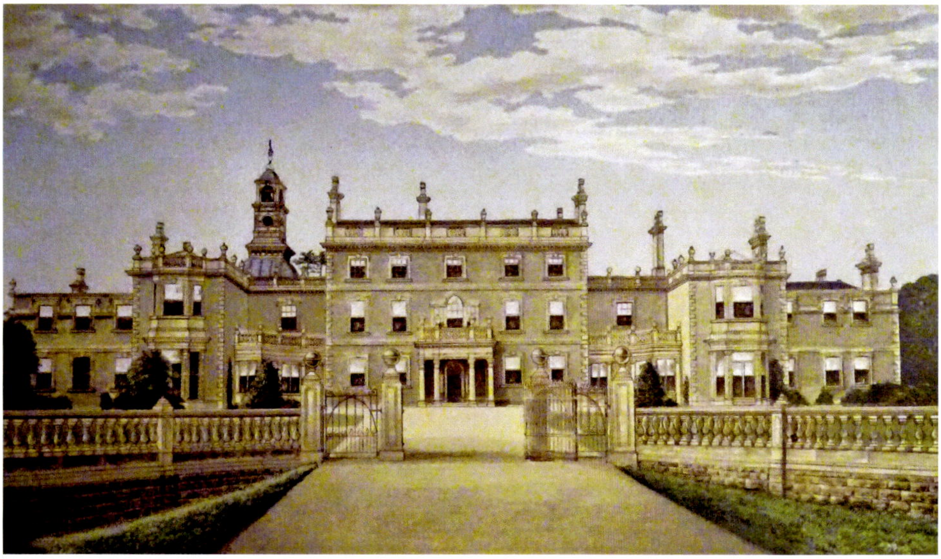

Bulwell Hall entrance front. From Morris's *Seats*. (M. Craven)

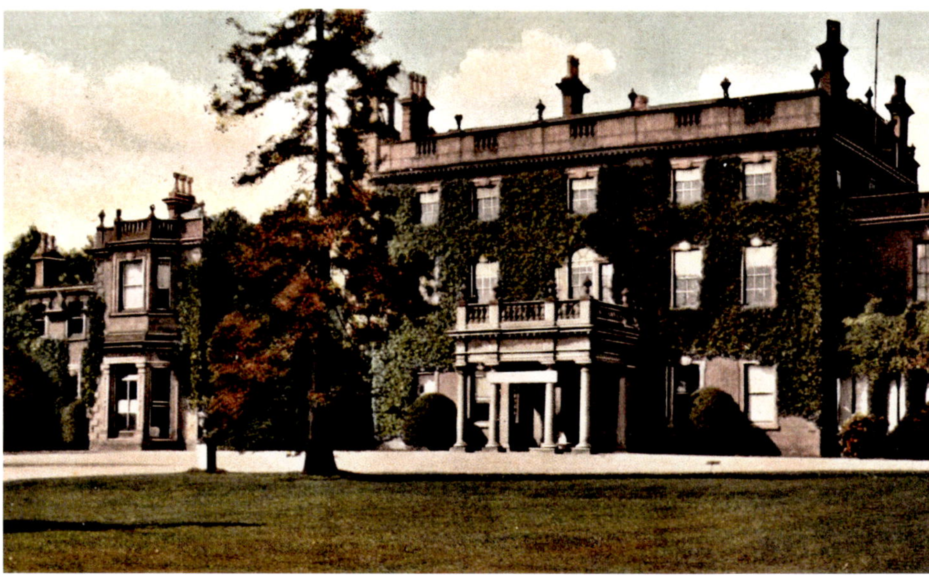

Bulwell Hall, from a chromolithographic postcard sent in 1910. (M. Craven)

Redhill Lodge, see below) for £85,000 to Alderman Sir Albert Ball, who conveyed it on to Nottingham Corporation at cost. As frequently happened, no satisfactory use could be found for such a large house, and after serving as a prisoner-of-war camp during the Second World War, it fell into desuetude and lay vandalised until demolition followed in 1958, leaving only stables and coach house.

55. Redhill Lodge, Arnold, 1958

Redhill Lodge was a Regency villa built on a small estate at Arnold by John Kirke (1796–1840), and his widow continued to live there into the 1860s. The brick and stucco house was of two storeys with a central pediment under a hipped roof with a entrance to the west side. An extension there housed a gallery for Mr Kirke's collection of paintings. In around 1866, it was bought by Nottingham solicitor Francis Burton (1814–92) who rebuilt the garden front with two wide canted bays and on whose death it passed by marriage to Revd E. M. Vaughan, vicar of St Paul, Daybrook, who let it to Dr G. Elder. In 1895, the house and modest estate were bought by Thomas Hardy, and his son Revd T. B. Hardy had it in trust, living there until his death in 1904, his wife Mary Ann surviving him until 1907. The estate then passed to Thomas's sons John Henry Hardy (1866–1937) and Charles and, as with Bulwell (see above), and it was sold in 1908 for £78,262 to Sir Albert Ball from whom, similarly, it came to Nottingham Corporation. The house and land were later transferred to the Air Ministry, but in 1958 both it and Bulwell were declared redundant and sold for redevelopment as housing, both houses being unceremoniously demolished.

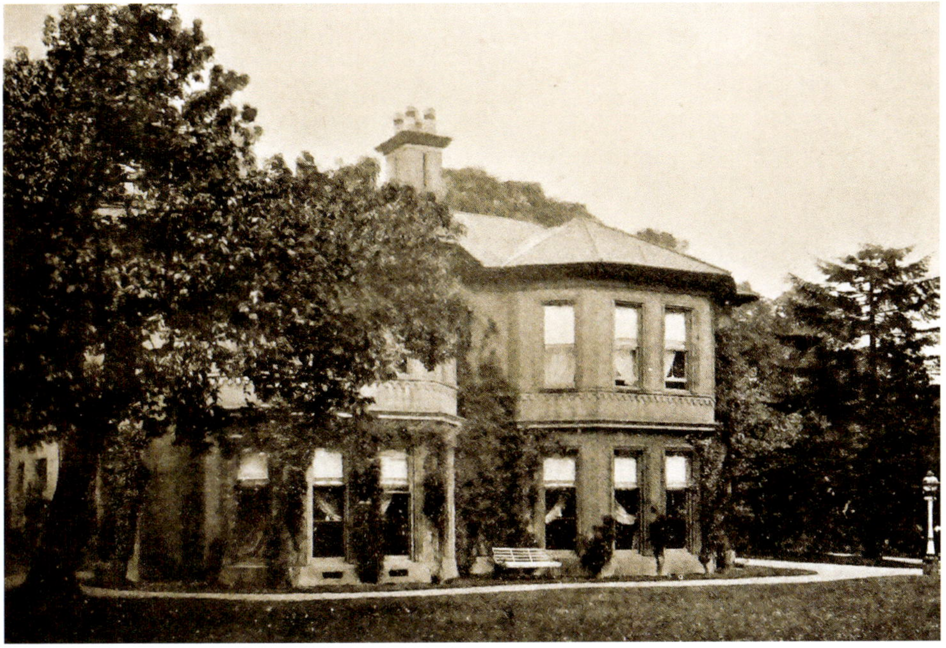

Red Hill Lodge garden front, 1901. (Bamfords Ltd)

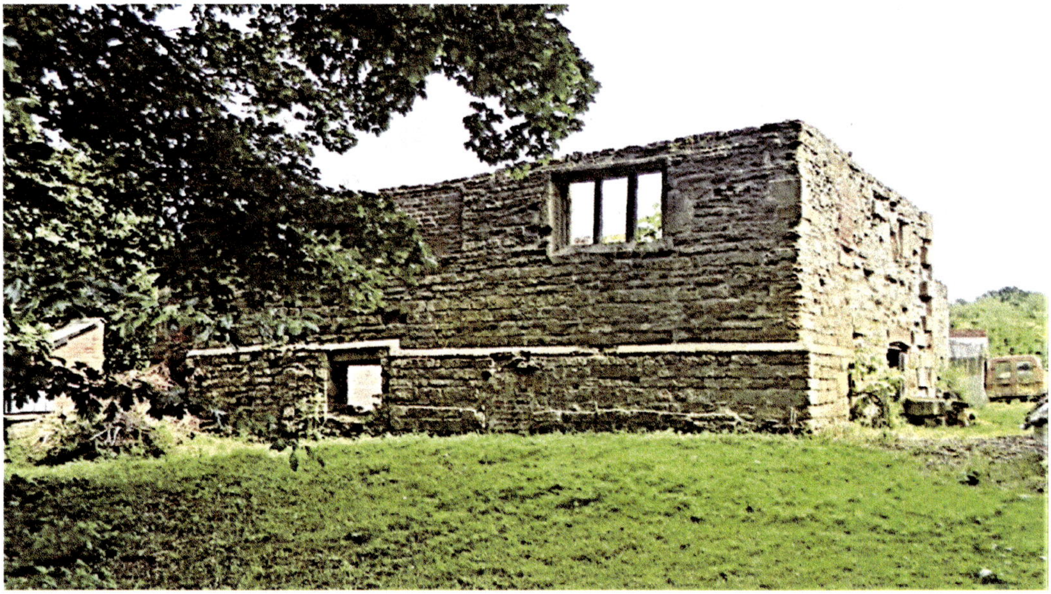

Wansley Hall standing remains, 2018. (Rob Howl, CC BY-SA 2.0)

56. Wansley Hall (II and SAM), 1960

The ruins of this important medieval sandstone-built house of twelfth-century origins, mainly now show fabric fifteenth-century date. The layout appears to have been T plan, as at Skegby (see p. 36) and elements of earlier phases are detectable, including the two-storey great hall, but the southern wing is later. There was a domestic chapel, the site probably marked by the adjacent Chapel field. Ralph de Wandesley held it in 1279 in succession to his forebears, but his daughter and heiress, Isabel, brought it by marriage to William de Gratton of Grattton (Derbyshire), who died in 1339. The estate seems to have extended to around 3,000 acres. Wiliam de Gratton's son left three daughters after which the estate, much diminished by partition, eventually came to the Middletons, who rebuilt the house. In the mid-sixteenth century, they were followed by their heirs the Howitts, who sold up as a result of the Civil War, by which time the estate had been reduced to a single farm. The hall was consequently reduced and simplified to function as a farmhouse, but deteriorating fabric and a fall of masonry caused its abandonment in 1960 and the roof was removed, leaving a shell which was consolidated in 1987.

57. Calverton Hall (II), 1961

Calverton Hall was a stuccoed Regency villa, of two storeys under a hipped roof, of three wide bays with a six-bay return and a band between the storeys, built 1818-19. About a decade later, the garden front acquired two single-storey wings set some 10 feet forward of the main façade to provide more reception space, each containing a ceiling of considerably greater height than those in the main block and these additions were connected by a colonnade of paired Ionic columns. At the same time an extension weas added to the north, thus turning a villa into what was effectively a country seat of some pretension. The client for all this – by an unidentified architect – was General Sir John Coape Sherbrooke GCB (1764–1830), former Governor-General of British North America 18712–18, third son of William Coape of Arnold, whose elder son was the heir of the Oxton estate (see p. 64) in 1754. Sir John left no issue but, unlike the Oxton estate, Calverton did not pass to the colonel's Lowe (later Sherbrooke) cousins, but to Captain William Henry Oates, grandson of Samuel Oates of Chapel Allerton, Yorkshire, and the general's sister Sarah (who had died in 1834). As Oates later inherited his father's house near Newark, followed by a brief tenancy in the early 1850s of Lady Sherbrooke, the house was let to John S. Wheatley, a lace manufacturer (recorded there in 1864), who in due course also died unmarried, in this case in 1888. When his sister died, the Oates family sold house and modest estate to Frank Evelyn Seely TD, JP, DL (1864–1928), third son of the industrialist Sir Charles Seely, 1st Bt of Sherwood Lodge (see p. 88). but in 1914 the Ecclesiastical Commissioners purchased it as a vicarage, which use lapsed in the 1950s, and in 1961 it was sold and demolished to build a miners' welfare institute, since succeeded by a housing estate.

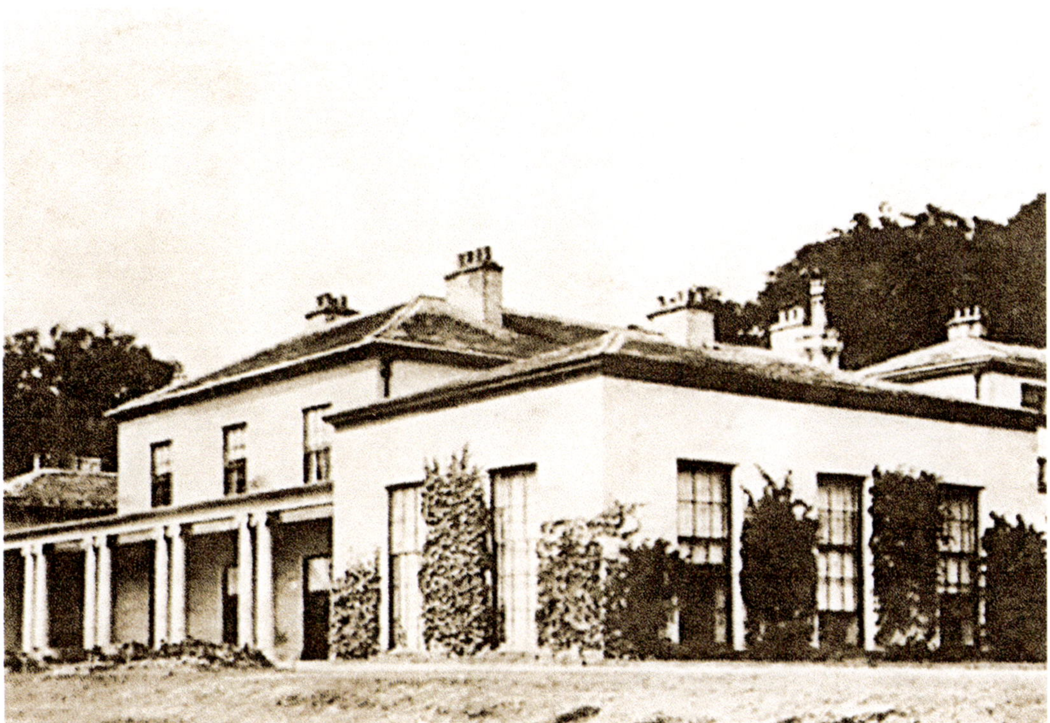

Calverton Hall from the south-east. From a postcard sent in 1908. (M. Craven)

58. Watnall Hall (II*), 1962

Watnall Hall was one of the most handsome late seventeenth-century houses in the county, and its demolition in 1962 was a serious loss. Not that it was the first house on the site, for the Rollestons seem to have built a house there in the second decade of the seventeenth century, of which the later house was nominally a reconstruction, reflected in its H plan and which was completed in 1692. The fine two-storey garden front of eight bays returned east to form a seven-bay entrance front with a recessed five-bay centre, the doorcase being ensigned by a segmental pediment carried on Ionic half columns. The north contained elements of the previous house, and the west was rebuilt in the early eighteenth century. The entrance court was closed from the 1720s by an iron railing punctuated by a superb pair of gates with armorial overthrow by Robert Bakewell of Derby, which was later moved to beside the (surviving) lodge on the main road and seems now to be lost. The interior featured two panelled and pilastered rooms, much rich plasterwork attributable to Samuel Mansfield of Derby and a superb timber staircase, the rail being supported on one turned and two twisted balusters per tread with enriched tread ends. The Rollestons had inherited from a younger branch of the Binghams of Bingham in the sixteenth century, John Rolleston

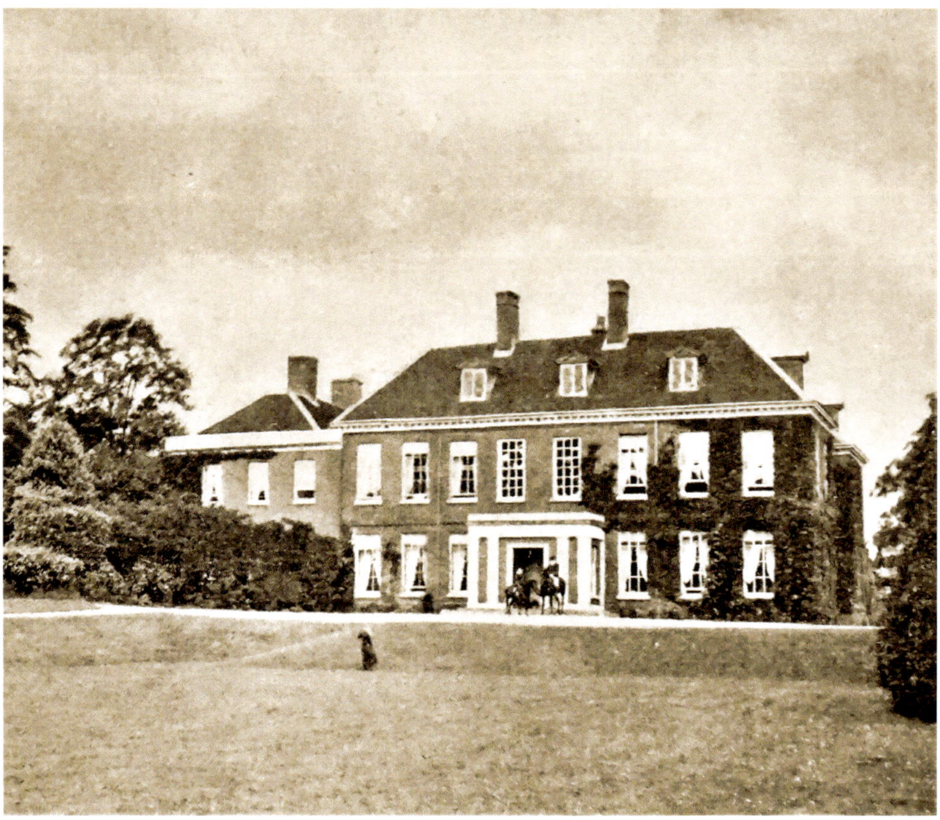

Watnall Hall south front, 1900. From Briscoe. (M. Craven)

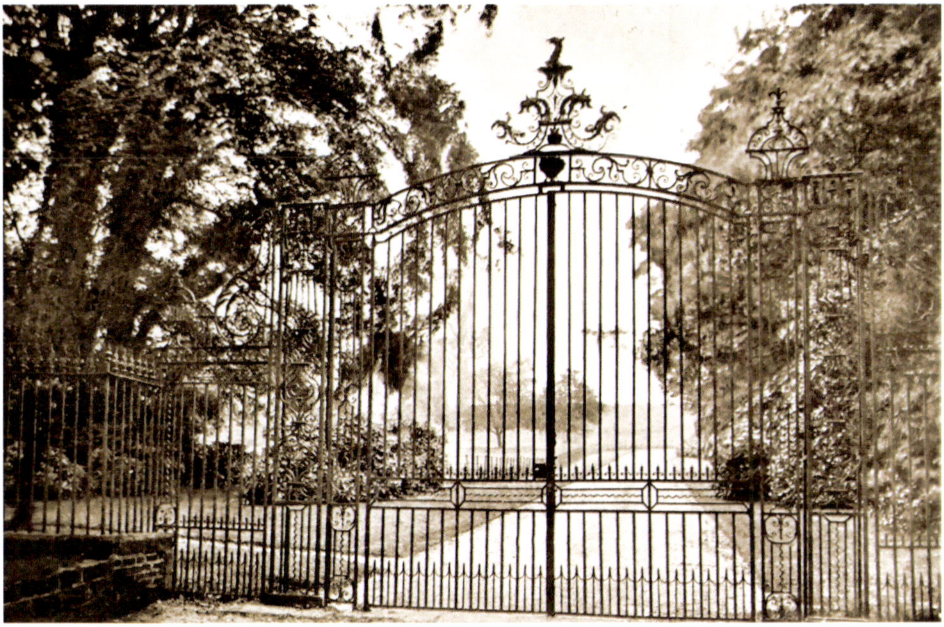

Watnall Hall's Bakewell gates in decay, 1900. From Briscoe. (M. Craven)

(d. 1637) having built the first house, its successor being the work of his nephew and, in 1685, ultimate heir Edward Rolleston. In the mid-nineteenth century Henry Burstall was tenant. The future of the house was plunged into doubt after the death without issue of Colonel Sir Lancelot Rolleston KCB, CBE, DSO, TD, DL (1847–1941) and in 1962 it succumbed to demolition. Ten years after its tragic loss, a housing development called Rolleston Crescent was built across the site – the final indignity.

59. Ossington Hall (II), 1963

In 1727–28 the Tudor hall at Ossington was replaced by George Cartwright, who built a well-proportioned plain, stone-fronted two-storey house with dormers, the garden front of which extended through nine bays with a three-bay breakfront under a plain parapet. The entrance front was similar but pedimented and flanked by two substantial pavilions forming a courtyard and joined by arcaded links, somewhat in the manner of James Gibbs, but perhaps lacking his surer touch. In 1768 William Denison, a successful Yorkshire woollen merchant bought the estate. After his death in 1782, his brother Robert commissioned the (then) seemingly ubiquitous William Lindley of Doncaster in 1788–90 to make considerable additions and improvements. After he had died, his nephew and heir John Denison (formerly Wilkinson) decided to enlarge on these, too, bringing in Sir John Soane for the purpose in 1805, to extend the flanking pavilions through to the garden front where they featured open pediments and blind niches. He also made alterations to the interior. It was further altered in 1839–40 by 1st Viscount Ossington

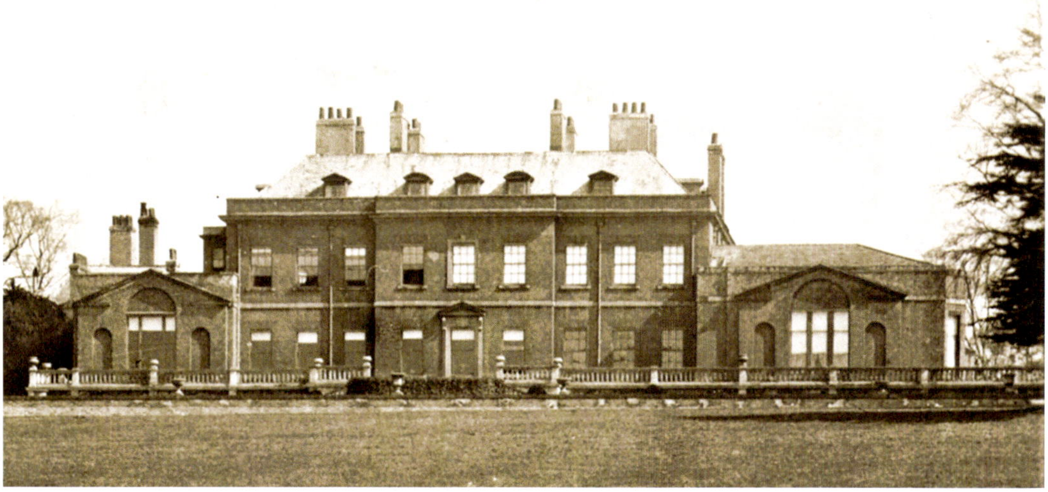

Ossington Hall entrance front. From a postcard sent in 1905. (M. Craven)

(Mr Speaker Denison) and the estate has remained with the Denison family since. The house went in 1963 but the parkland and gardens (improved by W. A. Nesfield), although largely reverted to wilderness, nevertheless remains unspoilt, and contain John Carr's domestic chapel (1782), also the sundial, main gates and a delightfully fanciful well head cupola with fishscale canopy by J. B. Philip of 1877, a memorial to Edward Denison (d. 1870).

60. Wilford Grange, Wilford, Nottingham (II), 1964

It is believed that the house which subsequently (and vicariously) acquired the name Wilford Grange became the subject of a rent charge for the relief of the poor of Nottingham under the terms of the will of Sir Thomas Manners in 1562. Subsequently, the house is said to have been rebuilt in the early seventeenth century by Gervase Handley, whose family later moved to Chilwell. In the later eighteenth century it seems to have acquired a two-and-a-half-storey range, which was suffered to remain in 1818 when Robert Leeson decided to replace the ancient house with a new, stone-built, two-storey, five-bay Regency villa with a curved bow on the narrow west end. Before 1824, he also added a further range to the south-east angle in matching style, masking the end bay of the original façade. The interior was of good quality, the staircase having stick balusters and a wreathed mahogany rail. There were 2 acres of landscaped grounds which included the eighteenth-century Orchard Cottage. Later in the nineteenth century it was tenanted by William George Cursham, a solicitor from *c.* 1850 to the 1880s, then by Sydney Thomson, a silk merchant, followed by Judge William Masterman at the turn of the century, after which the Leesons moved back in for a time before selling to the Bates family. Mrs Bates turned the house very tactfully into flats in the 1950s, but on her death in December 1962 the executors decided to sell for redevelopment. It was consequently vacated in 1963 and, despite the entreaties of

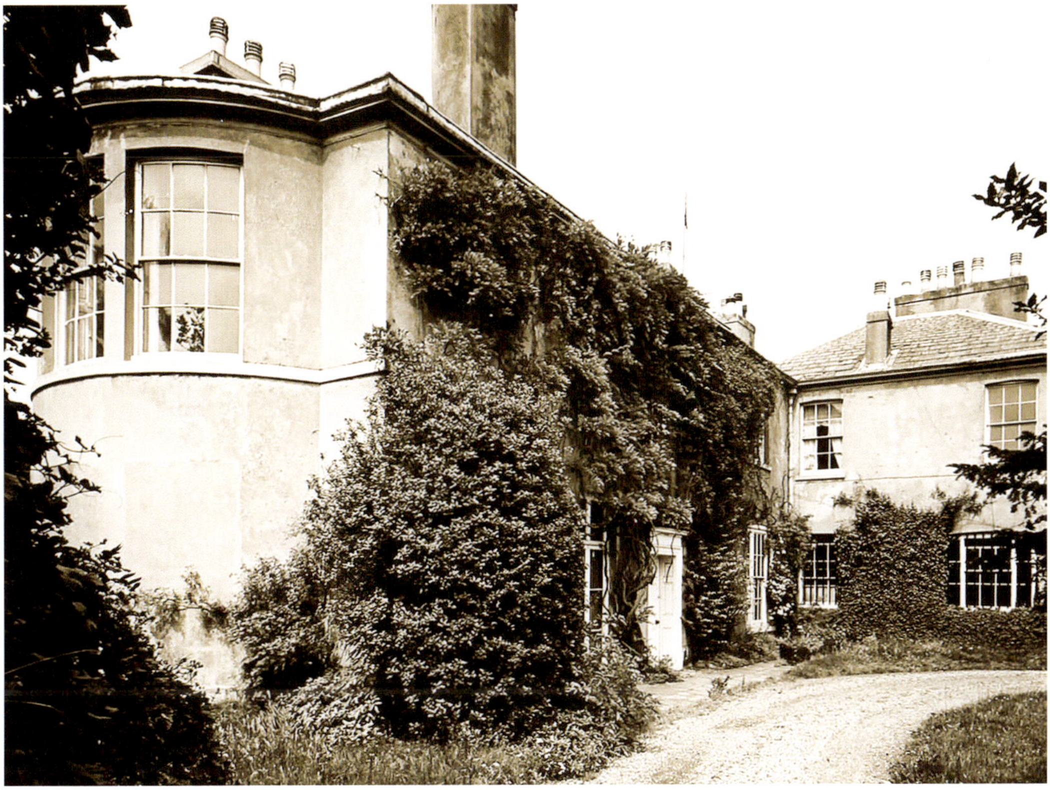

Wilford Grange entrance front from the south-west, 1963. (National Monument Record/ Historic England Archive)

the Georgian Group and others, Nottingham City Council's planning committee decided to allow its demolition on 14 May 1963; it was gone eight months later and the site is now marked by Grange Close (including Orchard Cottage).

61. Muskham Grange, North Muskham (II*), 1964

The history of the manorial estate at North Musklham from the time of Geoffrey Alselin in 1086 is complex, but in 1771 Earl Fauconberg was granted over 300 acres there through an enclosure award, but the estate of North Muskham Grange was held by lease from the manor and was long with the Marshall family. Lord Fauconberg soon disposed of his land to the Duke of Newcastle and banker Joseph Pocklington took over the lease (held of one of the Southwell Prebends) in 1775 from Bryan Cooke who had acquired it from the headmaster of Newark Grammar School. Pocklington immediately set about rebuilding an existing house in his inimitable style, producing a Palladian east front of two storeys and three bays, with a central pedimented breakfront and plat band. The façade was further enlivened by a pair of single-storey open-pedimented pavilions. He called it The Grange, and the work cost £398 9*s* 6*d*. By 1793 he had left for Muskham House and The Grange passed from John Battell to topographer William Rastall

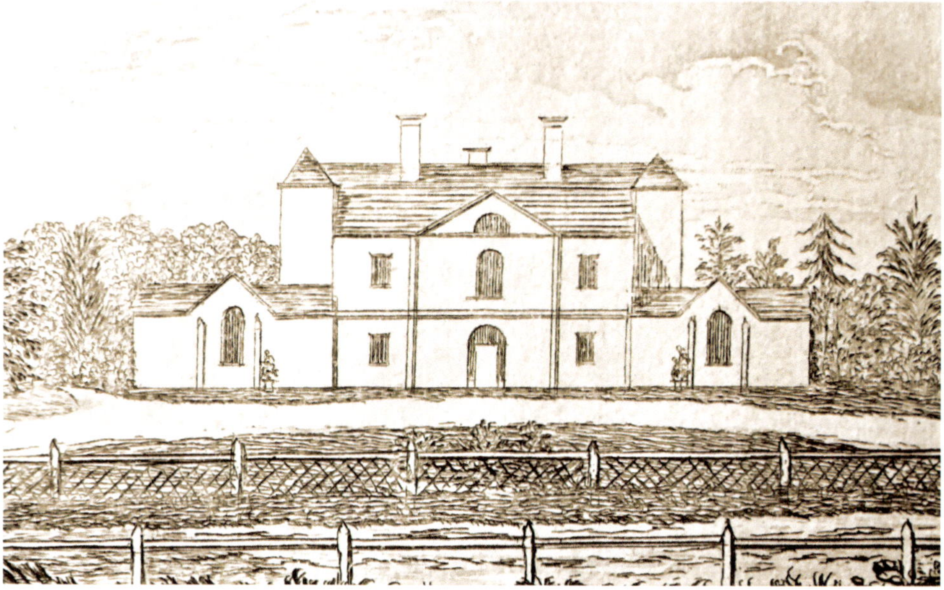

Muskham Grange east front, as depicted by Throsby, 1796. (M. Craven)

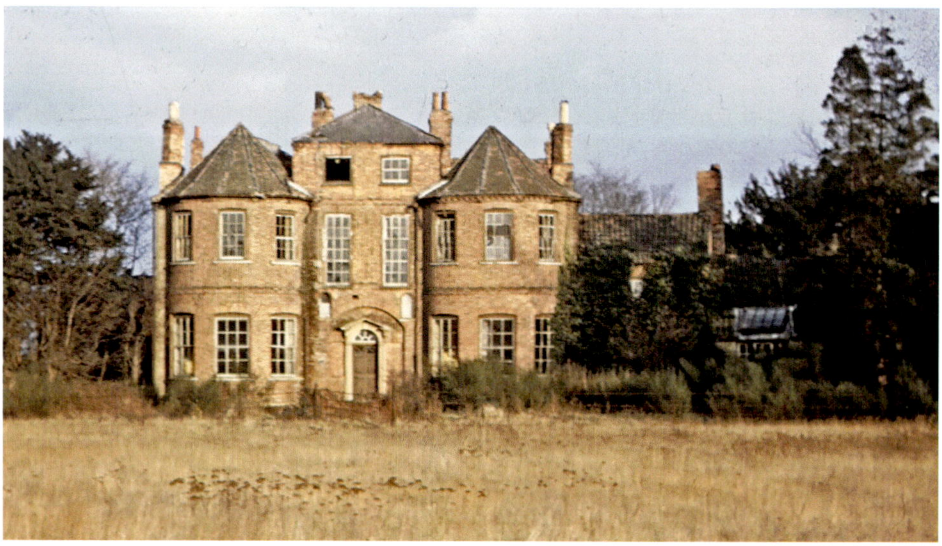

Muskham Grange west front in decay, November 1963. (B. Pollard)

Dickinson JP (1756–1822) who rebuilt the returns to widen the west front, flanking the east front with a pair of small towers. The central two bays of the six-bay west front were given a raised attic, a Doric entrance set in a blind arch, all crowded by two full-height curved bows with steep hipped roofs – by no means an improvement aesthetically. He later let the house to John Handley and P. Handley was there in 1872, but the Edges of Strelley acquired it shortly afterwards. It continued thereafter to be let to a variety of tenants. Unfortunately, most of the grounds were acquired through a CPO for the widening of the A1(T) in 1961, leaving the house virtually uninhabitable and it was demolished in the teeth of opposition in 1964.

62. Kirkby Old Hall (II*), 1964

The old hall at Kirkby was long the seat of the Kirkby family, but in the 1470s Richard Kirkby's daughter and heiress Agnes married William Sacheverell of Ible and Snitterton in Derbyshire. A century later, their descendant, Thomas Sacheverell of Brookhill Hall, Pinxton died leaving two daughters the elder of whom brought the ancient house (by then essentially long part of the Brookhill estate) to Richard Coke of Trusley (also Derbyshire) who probably enlarged an earlier house built by the Kirkbys on an ancient site. The entrance front had a large late fifteenth-century cross-wing to the west side and an earlier lower one to the east, both with close-studded timber framing latterly with stucco below the bressumers. The entrance was offset to the east, originally giving into a great hall, later divided both horizontally and vertically. The west side, close studded over a Medieval ground floor stone plinth, boasted an impressive stone chimney breast, and to the north all was older and lower. The end gables boasted mullioned and transomed fenestration, but only an earlier mullioned one between. The interior had a fine set of contemporary oak panelling, now happily removed to Trusley village hall. The house was tenanted from the later seventeenth century (in 1864 by Thomas Horsley), latterly as three flats, but had become very decayed by 1961 when the council declared it unfit. Efforts to sell it were fruitless and it was recorded by RCHM (E) and demolished in 1964.

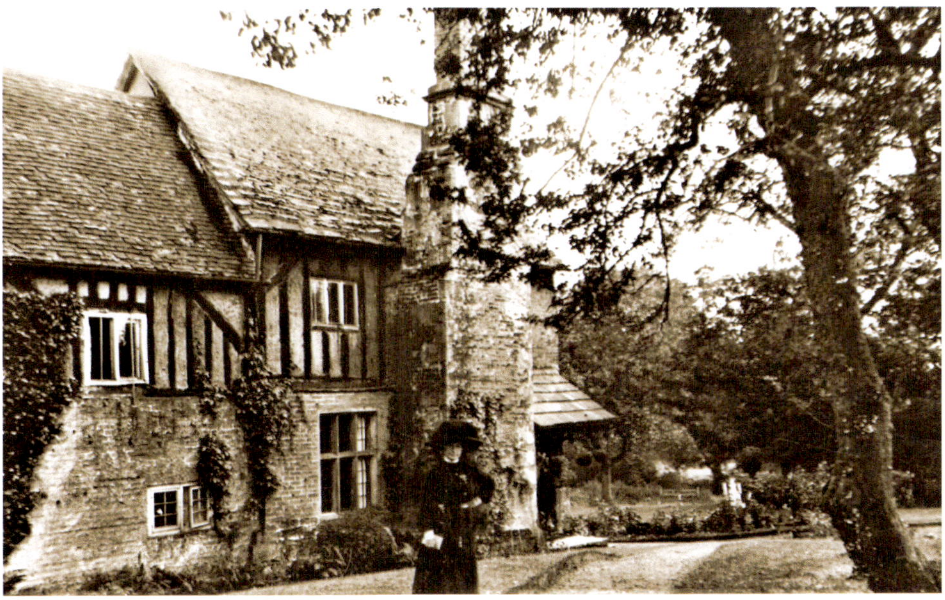

Kirkby Old Hall west front. From a postcard sent in 1913. (M. Craven)

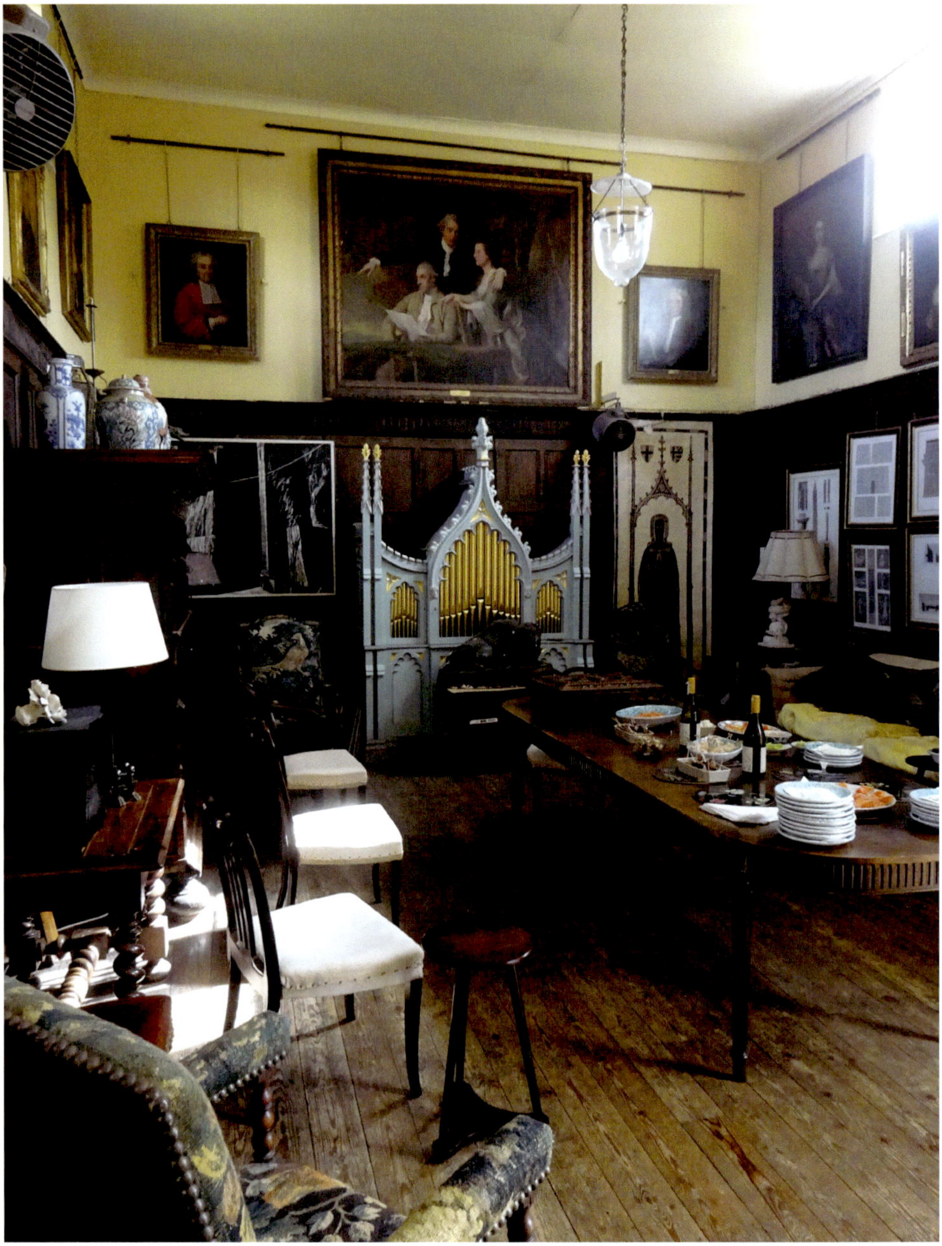

Kirkby Old Hall's sixteenth-century panelling in Trusley parish room, 2024. (M. Craven)

63. Thorney Hall (II), 1964

The Mering family had a house at Thorney from the later fourteenth century, having inherited the estate from the d'Aubeneys in 1387. In 1566, George Nevile, who had inherited Grove in the right of his wife, the sister of Sir John Hercy, bought Thorney from the Merings and he may well have rebuilt or replaced the house, which his descendant Edward Nevile entirely replaced, probably in the late 1730s, shortly after marrying. The traditional date is '*c.* 1750' but the handsome and well-proportioned house is in the plain manner of Francis Smith of Warwick, having two storeys with an attic above the cornice, the entrance front (of five bays) having the attic interrupted by a bold pediment with *oeuil-de- boeuf* over a Serlian window, whereas the garden front of seven bays was plain, all windows having rusticated stone lintels. There were superimposed Serlianas of the returns, suggesting some alterations under the errant guidance of Joseph Pocklington, for Edward's son, Colonel George Nevile (1739–1806). From 1877 the house was let to the Huttons of Gate Burton in Lincolnshire, of whom Major George Hutton DSO made alterations just prior to the First World War. In 1915 the house became a hospital for wounded soldiers but after the sale of much of the 650-acre estate, E. F. Nevile (1876–1945) resided there, but after his death it was little used and began to decay, being sold with what was left of the estate in 1963 and the house (bar part of the service wing) was demolished the following year. A new house has subsequently been built on the site.

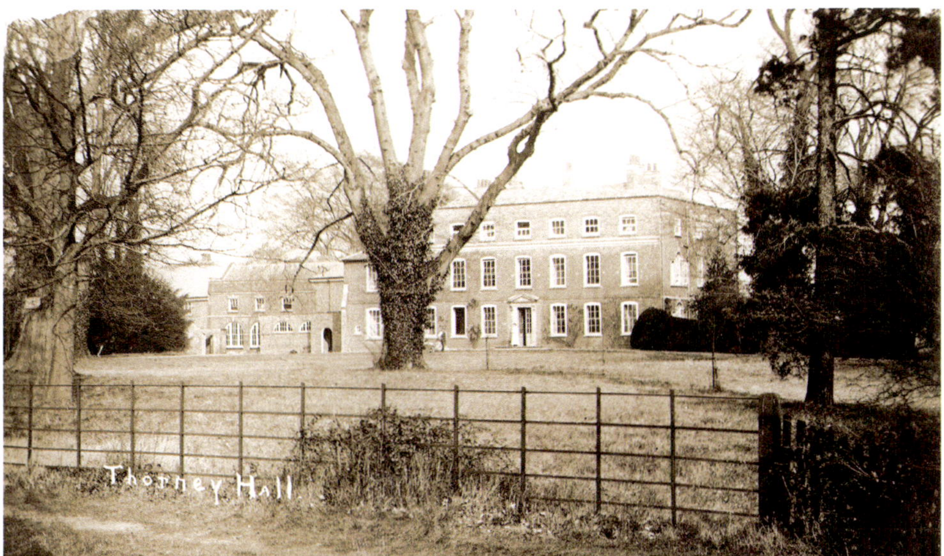

Thorney Hall garden front and part of the park, *c.* 1904. From a postcard. (James Darwin)

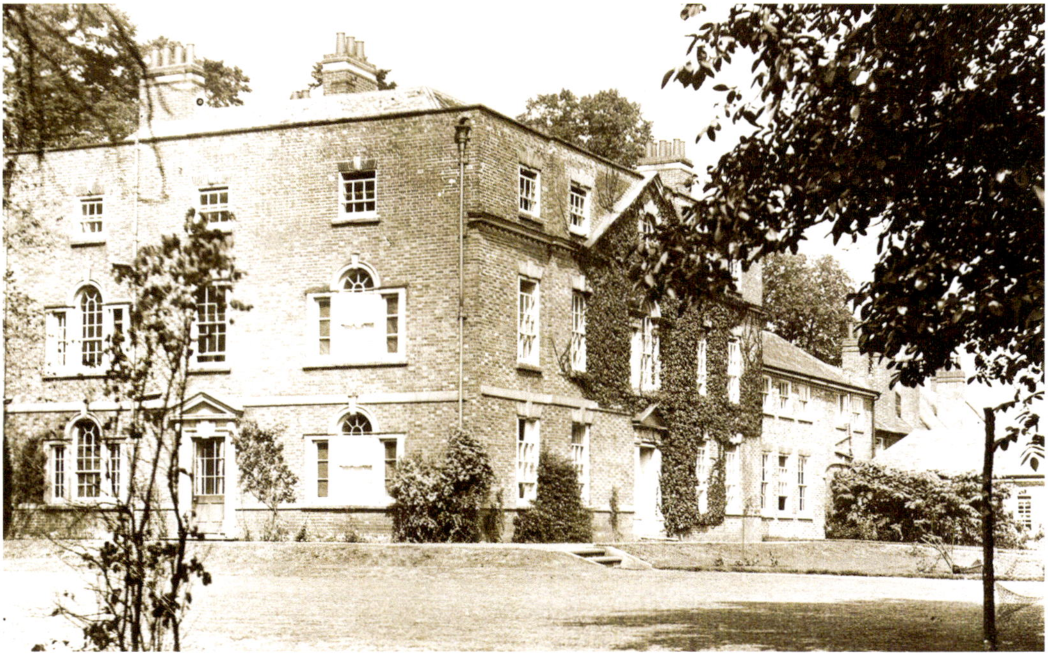

Thorney Hall entrance front, *c.* 1905. From a postcard. (James Darwin)

64. Whatton Manor (II), 1964

The year 1964 was a black one for Nottinghamshire country houses, for that year saw the loss also of Victorian Whatton Manor. The main estate at Whatton had descended through several distinguished families until the Gascoignes sold it in the sixteenth century to Sir Thomas Stanhope, and whose descendants, the earls of Chesterfield much increased their acreage through enclosure. By the 1790s Mr Hall of Nottingham owned some land here and his descendant, the upwardly mobile barrister Thomas Dickinson Hall (his mother a Dickinson of North Muskham, see p. 73), began acquiring more land to build up an estate – eventually 3,000 acres – to support the house he built during 1838–41. This was an aggressively symmetrical essay in Jacobethan, said to have been by Anthony Salvin, but perhaps lacking the excitement Salvin could bring to a building. It was of two storeys, with five-bay entrance and garden fronts under three straight coped gables, and three-bay returns with end gables only, the windows being mainly eight-light mullioned and transomed ones, with a central oriel over the arcaded entrance and canted bays to the garden fronts. There was a substantial service wing and a stable court. Hall died in 1879 aged seventy-one (outliving his son Cecil), and on his widow's death the grandson Montague (1870–1939) inherited, selling part of the estate to meet tax a decade later. He sold in 1919 to Samuel Chesterman, who in turn sold it on to William Goodacre Player of the Nottingham cigarette manufacturing family. He died in 1959 laving several sons, but his executors decided to demolish the house in 1964; the stable block remains.

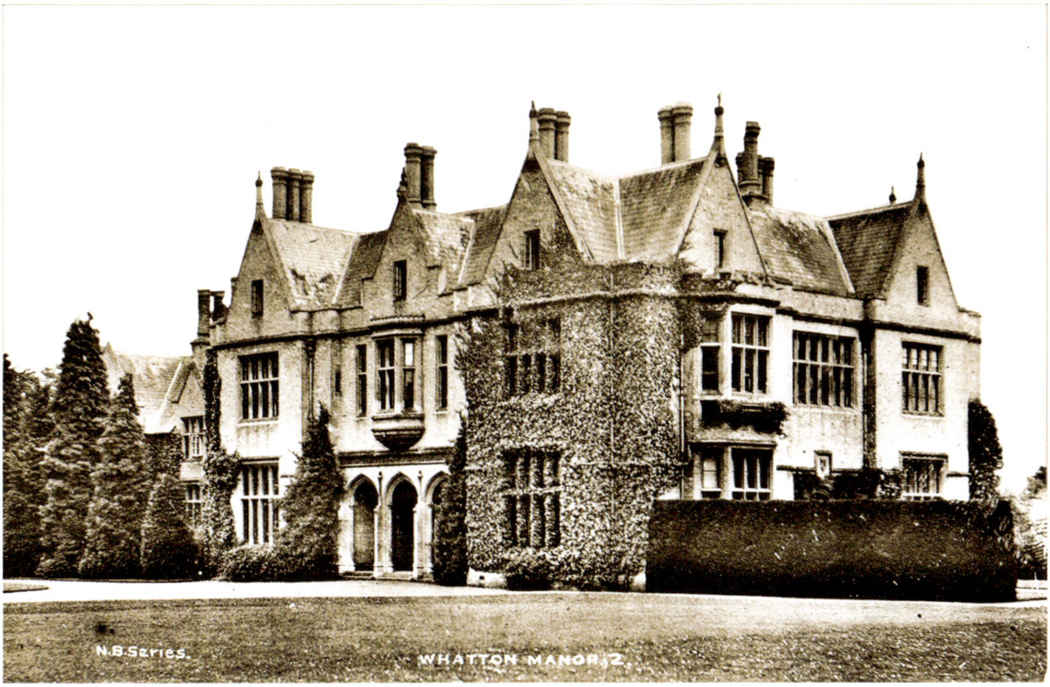

Whatton Manor entrance front, *c*. 1906. From a postcard. (James Darwin)

65. Sherwood Hall, Mansfield, 1965

Sherwood Hall was built in 1763–64 for Colonel John Kellett of the Royal Regiment of Horse Guards (The Blues) as a villa, not far from Mansfield and divided only by a belt of trees from the jurisdictional constraints of being within Sherwood Forest, although the dashing colonel originally named the house Shirewood Hall. Of brick, it was of two storeys with five bays of which the end ones and that in the centre were three-bay canted affairs, all under a parapet with balustraded sections over the bays. This arrangement also necessitated the placing of the entrance at bay two. There was only a single range behind the façade but a substantial service wing to the north-west with stables beyond. Kellett died in 1801, when his heirs sold the house and modest estate to Thomas Houldsworth (1771–1852), second son of Henry Houldsworth of Gonalston, of a family involved in cotton spinning, centered on Manchester. Thomas was also lord of the manor at Epperstone and sat as MP at first for Pontefract and later (hence his purchase) for North Nottinghamshire. In the event, he was only an occasional visitor, preferring to house his racing managers/trainers there, having provided suitable gallops on the estate. When he died unmarried in 1852, the property was sold to William Wilson whose heirs sold to the ubiquitous property developer, Sir Albert Ball, who let it in 1926 to Sir John Houfton (1857–1929) of Park Hall, Mansfield Woodhouse (see p. 92), then manager of the Bolsover Colliery and uncle of Arts and Crafts architect Percy Houfton (1873–1926), who designed Bolsover Model Village and may have worked at Sherwood Hall

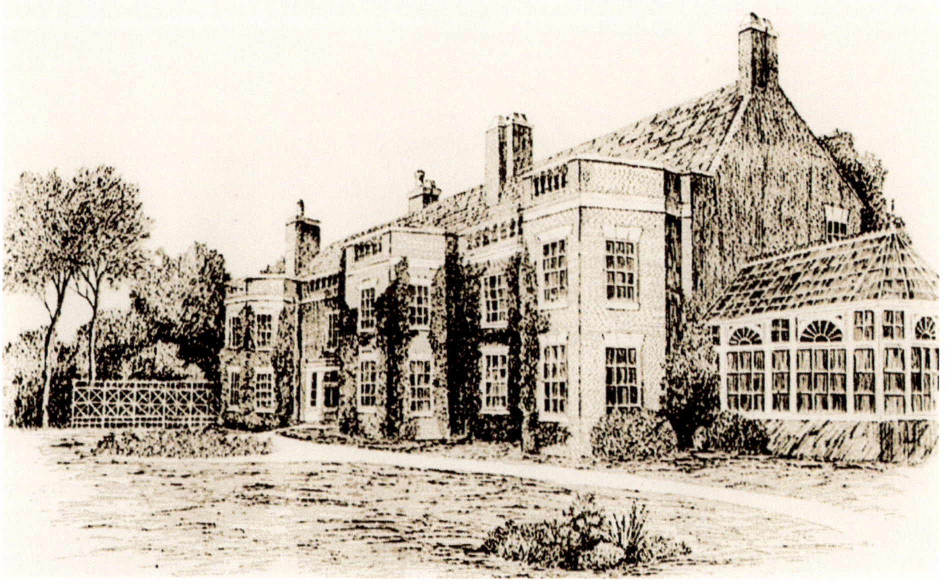

Sherwood Hall, from a twentieth-century drawing by J. Michael Hargreaves. (Private collection)

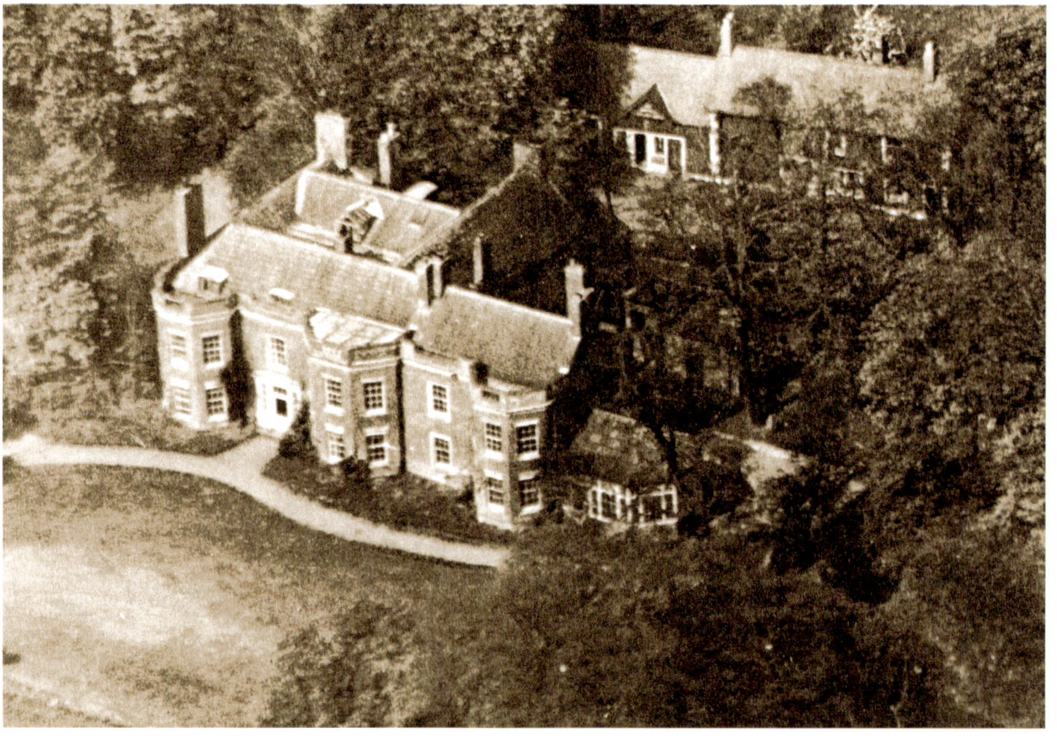

Sherwood Hall from the air, 1960s. (Mansfield DC)

(as it was by then called) too. He was followed in 1929 by Dr N. L. Tweedie but after he moved it was let as a school. It lay empty by the early 1960s, when it was bought and demolished in 1965 by a firm keen to build houses on the site.

66. Sutton Manor, Sutton Bonington (II), 1965

Sutton Manor – correctly, St Anne's Manor – was represented the capital mansion of one of the manorial estates into which Sutton Bonington became split. Its name, of course, derives from its proximity to the parish church, dedicated to St Anne. The house unwarrantably demolished in 1965 seems to have started out as a L- or U-plan timber-framed mansion, of which the right-hand cross-wing with its incongruous gable apex (later) stack seems to have been a survivor, latterly brick nogged and with timber casement fenestration. The central, great hall section had the entrance adjacent to the cross-wing, and two other bays, but with only vestigial timber framing remaining from a late seventeenth- or early eighteenth-century rebuild which also included the replacing of thatch with tile for the roof. The left-hand element was replaced at about the same period with an extension, breaking forward of the man façade, of two further bays, although the west gable end retained timber framing. The estate had long been with the Shirleys of Staunton Harold until Lord Tamworth (later 8th Earl Ferrers) sold the estate in 1832 to William Paget of the Nanpantan family who enlarged the house three decades later, although exactly how is unclear. In the later nineteenth century, the house was further subdivided into two parts and replaced by a Victorian villa nearby, but later still into four tenement cottages, but neglect by later freeholders

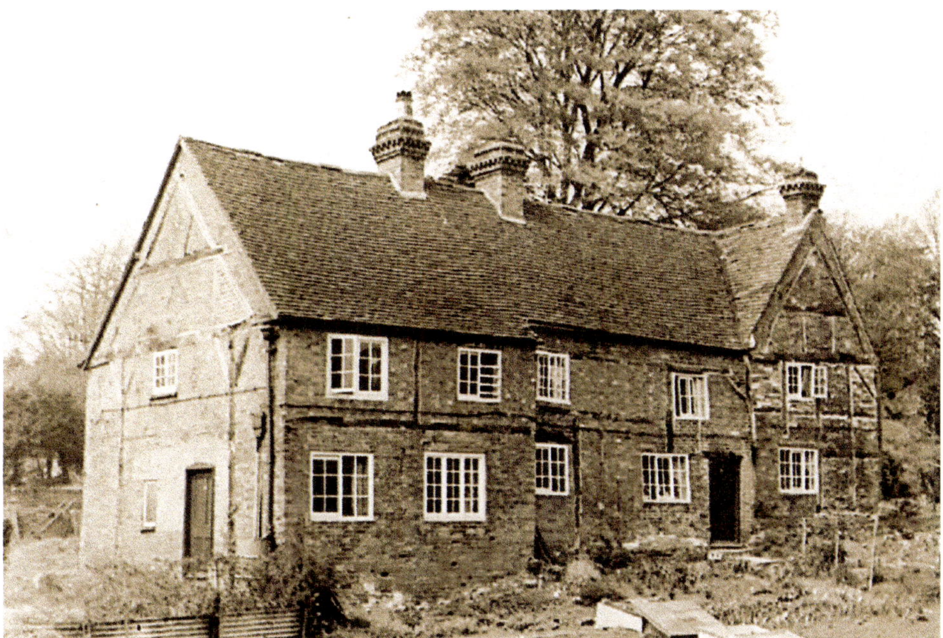

St Anne's Manor, Sutton Bonington, *c.* 1960. South-east view. (H. Jeffries)

led to them being declared unfit in 1961, and the house was demolished six years later.

67. Kirkby Hardwick, Kirkby-in-Ashfield (II), 1966

The estate here derives its name from the Hardwick family, who held it from at least the early twelfth century until 1240 when it passed to the Pierreponts of Holme. Whether the Hardwicks' house survived in use is by no means clear, however. In 1517, though, the estate was sold to George Talbot, 4th Earl of Shrewsbury, for £200 and there must have been a house on-site by then for it is thought that a substantial range was added to the house by Lord Shrewsbury shortly after purchase, including an outer wall and gatehouse. It is recorded that Cardinal Wolsey stayed there for a night in 1530 with his retinue. The estate subsequently passed to the Holles, dukes of Newcastle (who rebuilt it *c.* 1672), under whose heiress, Lady Oxford, in the mid-eighteenth century, much of the house was unroofed. She adapted the southern range as a four-bay three-storey farmhouse. In the early nineteenth century, the estate was involved in the property exchanges between the dukes of Newcastle and Portland, ending up with the latter. The coal measures stone-built Tudor house was of two storeys with attic gables above (as at Selston), lit by three- and four-light mullioned windows with four centered heads beneath cranked drip moulds and, like contemporary Longford Hall in Derbyshire, was embellished with a line of substantial external chimney breasts. The surviving wing was extensively rebuilt when the tenancy changed in 1853, and remained in use until after the First World War. It was ruinous in 1939, standing in the way of development the Summit Colliery adjacent to the west, ultimately succumbing to the demands of the nationalised coal industry under a

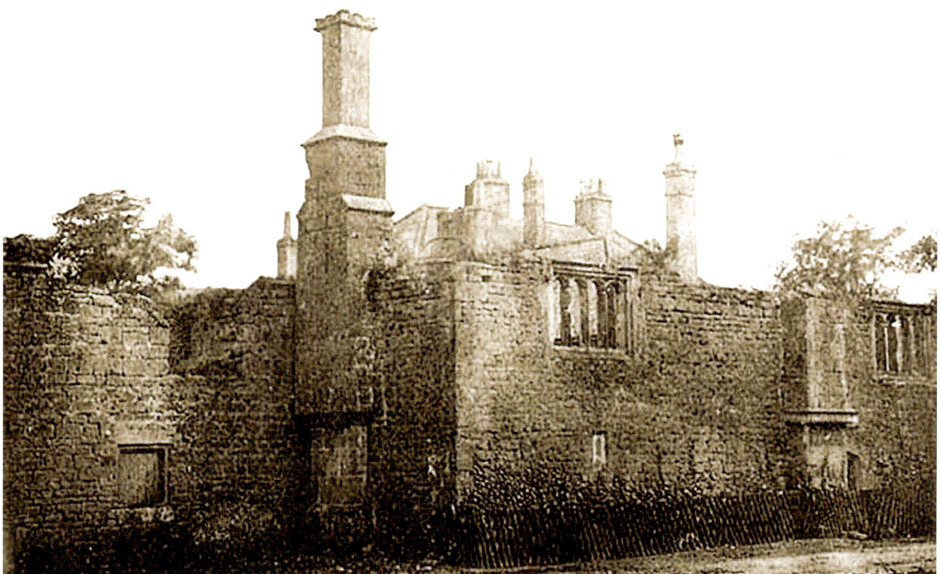

Kirkby Hardwick, the remains of the ancient house in 1912. (Thoroton Society)

CPO in 1966. Excavations by the Thoroton Society in 1880 and 2011–12 have much helped in understanding this enigmatic mansion.

68. Bramcote Hills (II), 1966

Bramcote Hills was an elegant brick two-storey Regency villa with a six-bay (south-west) garden front set at right angles to the entrance front, also of six bays, but graced with a substantial tetrastyle baseless Doric portico and all under hipped roofs. The north end of the entrance front was marked by a three-storey bay, set forwards and joined at the angle by a low attic, which looks very much like as smaller, earlier house incorporated into the villa. The three-bay west front included a conservatory and the stables were set on two sides behind. There were hipped roofs. The south front had a pediment over the central two bays, and the proportions look just slightly awkward, suggesting that the architect might well have been William Stretton of Nottingham, who had certainly worked in a municipal context for Alderman John Longden, the client, when he was mayor in 1807–08. While Longden was wealthy, he was also close kin to the even richer Sherwins and Gregorys and, indeed, his son John Sherwin Gregory (1803–69) was obliged to restyle himself as John Sherwin Sherwin following an inheritance in 1818, and in 1860 as John Sherwin Gregory on inheriting the Harlaxton estate. On his death, Bramcote Hills passed to his brother-in-law, the sixth son of Robert Holden of Nuthall Temple (see p. 44). From his son, Ernest Holden

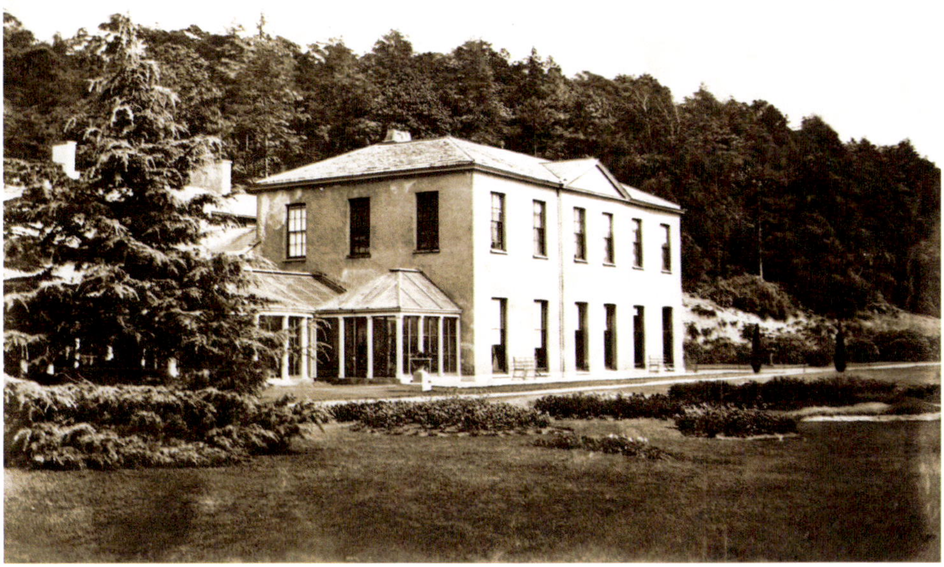

Bramcote Hills garden front, *c.* 1870. (James Darwin)

(1868–1937), house and estate passed to a cousin John Alfred Drury Lowe of Locko Park (Derbyshire), who let it to the FitzHerbert Wrights (of a Nottingham banking family), but during the war it became an hostel and rehabilitation centre. Post-war it became subject to a CPO for it to be incorporated into the Bramcote Hills School Campus and after a few years as flats for council employees, it was cleared away in 1969.

69. Bramcote Hall (II), 1966

In the mid-1830s, the Nottingham banker Ichabod Wright built a villa at Bramcote which Leonard Jacks later damned as 'Quaint not to say inconvenient'. It was inherited by his son, Charles Ichabod Wright, before the family moved to their large house at Mapperley in the 1850s, when Derbyshire baronet's son John Wilmot acquired it before selling to another Nottingham banker, Frederick Chatfield Smith MP (1823–1905). Smith was father to a large family (eventually there were eleven children) and he resolved to enlarge the house, which he did in spades, producing a neo-Jacobean monster in brick and stone, of two sprawling storeys with attics, embellished with a tower, a spire, a forest of chimneys not to mention canted and square bays – a riot of detail set on a series of terraces falling to a park of nearly 100 acres. Yet, for all that there was no estate as such. The architect may have been Henry Isaac Stevens of Derby, who worked with the Smiths elsewhere or George Robinson Isborne of London, who designed some of the family banks. Smith died in 1905 and his widow in 1914, and the family sold the house and grounds in 1920 to Trent College, which set up a feeder prep school there, which flourished until 1965 when it moved to fresh premises and the site was sold to the University of Nottingham which intended to set up a post-graduate centre there. This did not get underway immediately, and in 1966

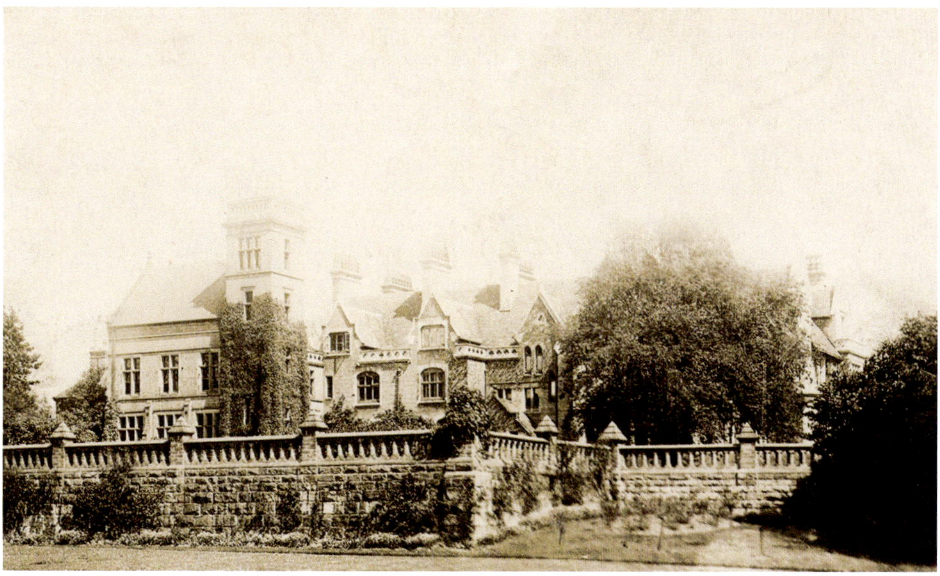

Bramcote Hall from the gardens, *c.* 1889. (James Darwin)

the building caught fire and burned out. The remains lingered on in diminishing proportions until 1972, although part of the parkland survives as a public park and a few courses of bricks from the building can still be seen.

70. Aspley Hall, Radford-on-Leen, 1967

A hunting lodge of the priors of Lenton had long stood here which, nearly two decades after the dissolution, was recorded as being in 'ruinous condition' but which contained a (great) hall, kitchen, and two parlours with chambers over. It was apparently timber framed but boasted a fifteenth-century brick three-stage tower with an attached newel staircase, containing the prior's solar chamber on the first floor. The estate, then called Aspley Woodhouse, came into the hands of the Blyth family, and from them to the Atkinsons before being acquired by the Willoughbys of Wollaton. No hint survives of what kind of structure the hall was by this time, but the Willoughbys soon settled their recusant cousins there, and even under George I, Francis Willoughby of Aspley was fined £48 *6s* 8*d* (£48.33) for adhering to his Catholic faith. His successor, Edward, seems to have been responsible for replacing the old house, although some considerable portions of it must have remained within – solar tower included – for neither of its three-storey brick-and-stuccoed main fronts (east entrance and south garden) was symmetrical, although both were of five bays of windows, most of which were endowed with inconsequential-looking cranked hood moulds. These façades pivoted around the creeper-clad stair tower of the former solar tower, itself incorporated into the south end bay of the east front, which accordingly broke forward noticeably, and behind the parapet of which was a confusing roofscape. The entrance was later disguised by a Victorian ground-floor addition, and the house was stuccoed. It was let to Belper born Richard Birkin (1805–70), of the lacemaking family and

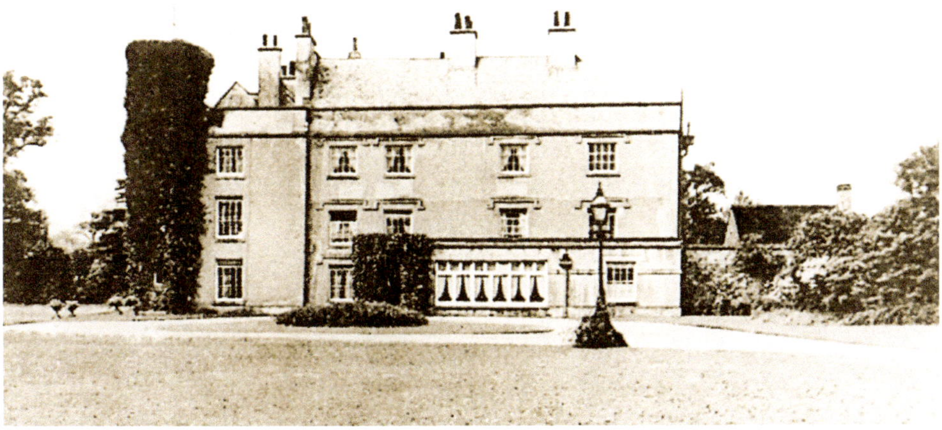

Aspley Hall entrance front. From the 1925 sale catalogue. (Private collection)

ultimately sold by the Wollaton estate in 1925 to Alderman George Taylor of Nottingham who occupied it until he died in 1965. The son was unable to find either use or buyer for the house and it was demolished in 1967 with a housing development replacing it the following year.

71. Coddington Hall (II), 1968

The house began as a relatively modest two-and-a-half-storey villa called Greenfield, erected by one of the Staffordshire coal-owning Colcloughs in around 1787 on land obtained from the Heron family, who had been awarded it under the Coddington Inclosure of 1760. The Colcloughs continued there until 1810 when it was sold to the Fisher family who appear to have renamed it Beaconfield House, although this may have been down to their tenant, Newark banker (and in 1836 mayor) Thomas Spragging Godfrey (1801–59). However, in or around 1832 the Fishers sold the freehold to James Thorpe (1791–1843), who shortly afterwards flanked the original house with projecting two storey wings joined by a colonnade across the entrance, extending on the return by five bays, the windows having sliding iron jalousies and the house a coat of Roman cement, grooved to resemble ashlar. Colonel James Thorpe, JP, DL (1823–1902) further enlarged it, adding a taller wing to the west and a low tower to the east in 1862–63. Major John Somerled Thorpe was killed on the Somme in 1916, whereupon the house was requisitioned by the army and later bought by the War Ministry, the colonel's brother settling in a new house on the estate and his son James (1905–39) moving south. In 1920, being surplus to requirements, it was for sale, failed to make its reserve but in 1922 the house and 13 acres were sold to Thomas Margerrison, who divided it, living in one part and renting the other

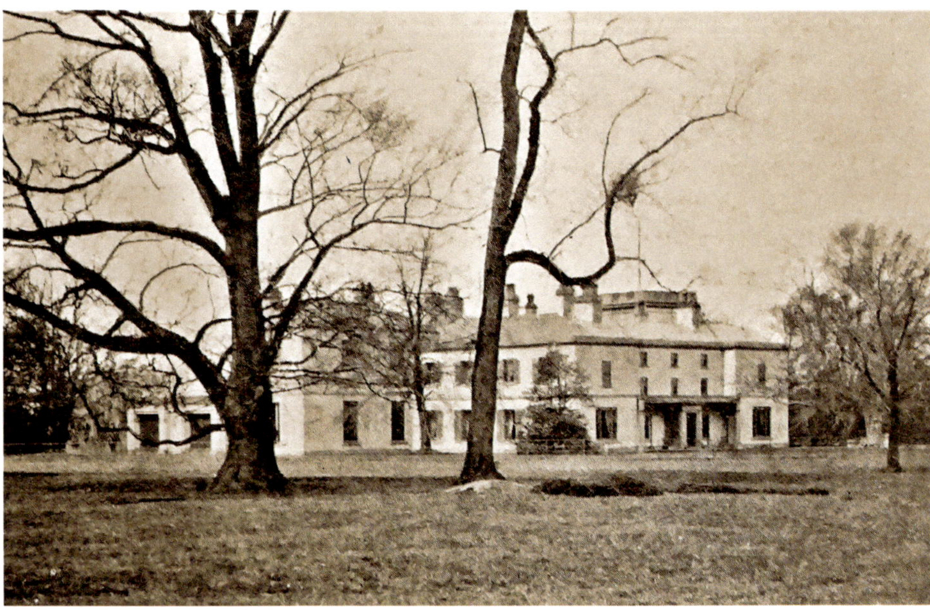

Coddington Hall from the south-west. From Briscoe, *c.* 1900. (M. Craven)

as prestige offices, latterly of the Anglo-Iranian Oil Co. In 1940, requisitioned again, it became the officers' mess and quarters of satellite bomber base, RAF Winthorpe, continuing in that role until 1962, when it was allowed to decay, the land sold for a housing development (ironically since itself replaced) and the last portion was cleared away in 1968.

72. Blyth Hall, 1972

After Lord Pembroke's mighty seat at Wilton, Blyth Hall was the first house to have raised corner pavilions, a conceit derived from influential Italian Renaissance architect Sebastiano Serlio (*c.* 1475–1554). The house has been firmly attributed to William Talman and was built in 1683-84 for Edward Mellish, a vintner whose family had acquired the estate, formerly part of Blyth Priory. This his forebear John Mellish had acquired from Sir Gervase Clifton to whom it had come via a the Stanhopes and Saundersons. The house, though, was much more compact than Wilton, with five bays between the towers, stone faced but with a rich interior, with plasterwork by Edward Gouge, especially in the staircase hall. William Mellish, in the century following, expanded the estate and made alterations, including rebuilding the pavilions with pyramidal roofs with chimney stacks at the apices. A generation on, John Carr, a close friend of William Mellish (who served lucratively as Receiver General of the Customs) was commissioned to enlarge the house, which he did with some tact between 1769 and 1782, adding a large drawing room between the north-west and north-east pavilions with a wide canted bay and a lavish Adam-esque interior, stables to the south, a bridge and much estate building of all kinds. The estate was sold in 1806 to Sheffield iron-founder Joshua Walker, whose

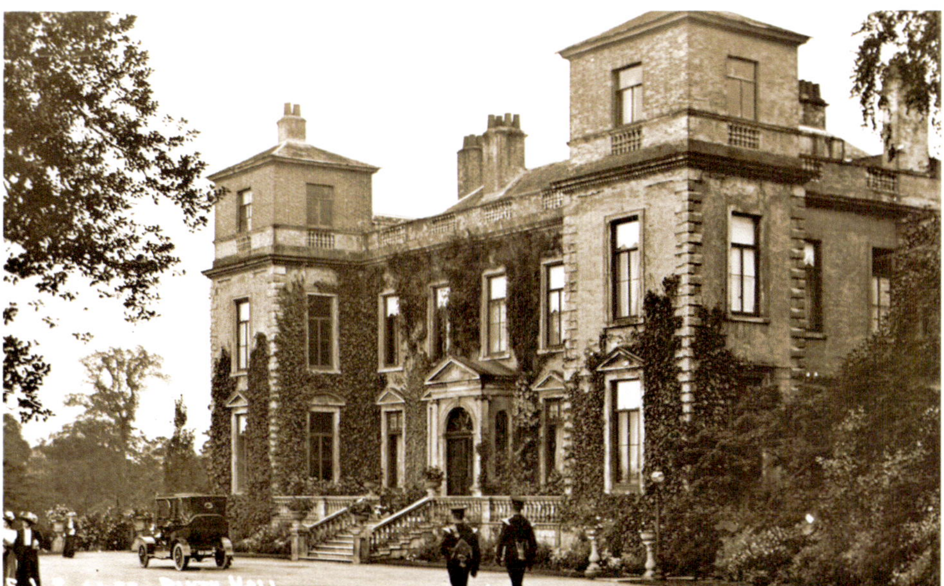

Blyth Hall entrance front, *c.* 1903. From a postcard. (M. Craven)

family remained in possession until 1889 when it was again sold to Francis Willey (1841–1929), later 1st Lord Barnby. On his death his son sold the house and by 1938 had become a vandalised shell, further wrecked by the military during the Second World War. The ruins were cleared for a housing development in 1972.

73. Sherwood Lodge, Arnold (II), 1973

Sherwood Lodge started out as a rather grand villa built for William Coape of Arnold and Farnah, Duffield, Derbyshire. Although said to date from 1790, it was almost certainly completed somewhat earlier by Coape for his eldest son William to occupy. Coape Sr was married to the residual heiress of the Sherbrookes of Oxton (see p. 64) whose surname he later assumed. More Palladian than Robert Adam, the main east front was of seven bays and two and a half storeys high with a central, rather abrupt pediment containing an *oeuil-de-boeuf* with the central bay consisting of a full-height blind arch enclosing entrance, a tripartite widow and a thermal window below the archivolt. There was a low parapet and a hipped roof. The south front was of three bays (one canted and of full height) and to the north five. The architecture suggests a local man rather than a national figure, perhaps Samuel Stretton of Nottingham or possibly William Henderson of Loughborough. Coape's elder son lived there until he inherited Oxton in 1799. He was followed by his brother Colonel Henry

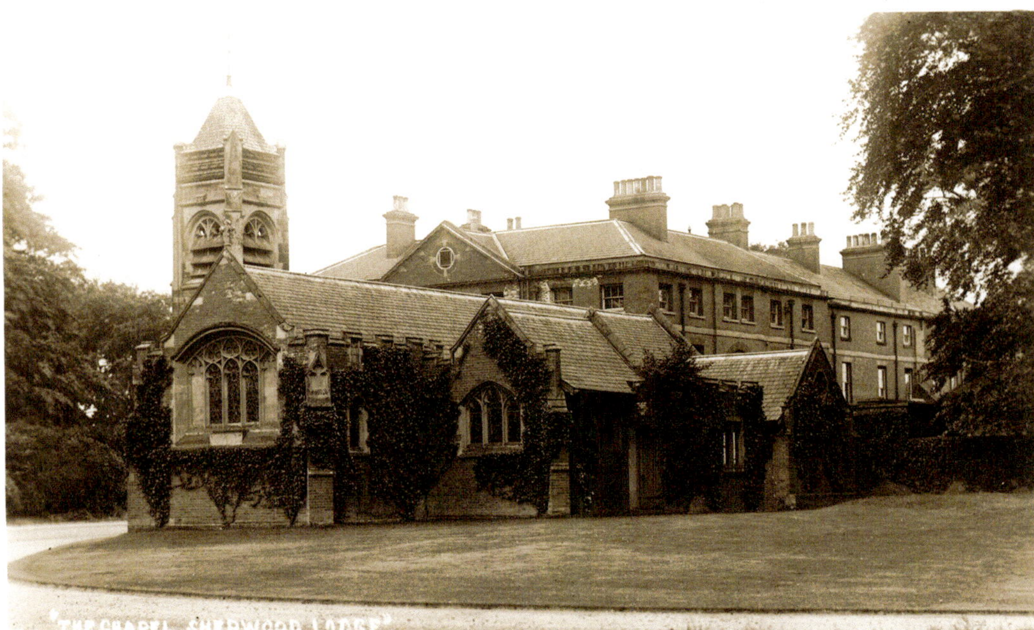

Sherwood Lodge and chapel (foreground), 1902. From a postcard. (James Darwin)

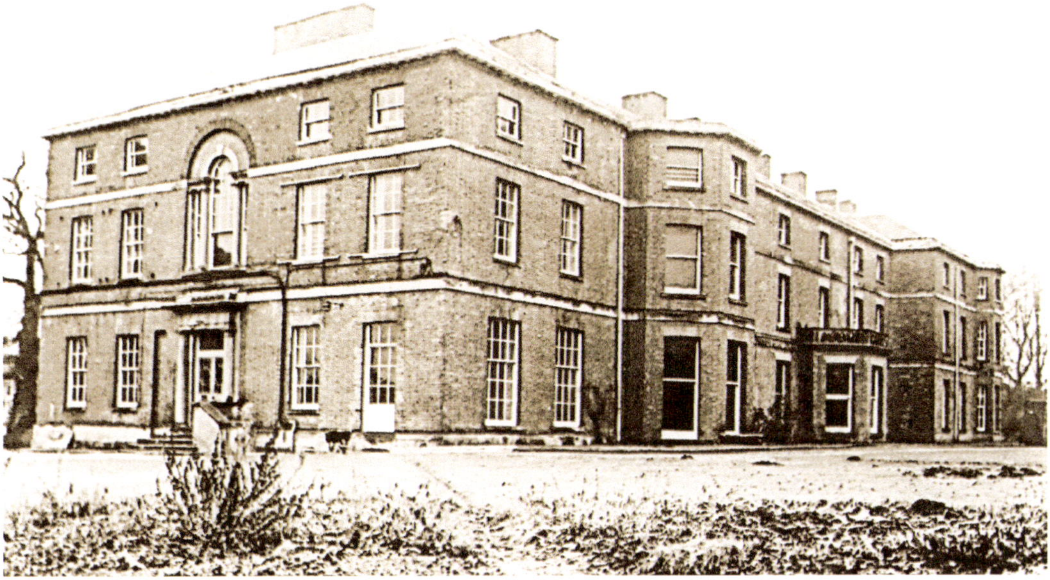

The long south front of Sherwood Lodge shortly before demolition, 1972. (Bamfords Ltd)

Coape, an active commander of the local militia unit, who in 1840 called in Derby architect Charles Humphreys (1819–75) to extend the house. Henry Coape (later Sherbrooke) never married and died in 1849, when the house was sold to Colonel Samuel Need (later Welfitt) of Langwith Lodge (widower of a daughter of the King of Oudh) who let it to the local sporting vicar of Arnold, Revd George Holcombe JP DL who held the cure of Arnold as a true squarson from 1812 to 1872. On his death, coal mining and property magnate Sir Charles Seely, 1st Bt (1833–1915), bought the estate to run with his sons at Calverton (rather as the Coapes had done) and set about greatly extending the house, very much in matching style, including an accomplished neo-classical west front which looks like the work of the same architect as Nos 14–22 Shakespeare Street, Nottingham, of similar date and almost echoes the entrance façade. The south front was elven bays with three canted bays making it seem a lot longer, and it terminated in a pretty conservatory by Messenger of Loughborough. In 1903 Sir Charles added a striking Arts and Crafts chapel flanking the east front by Sir Aston Webb, with interior decoration of high quality by H. W. Lonsdale. The Seelys also built up the estate extending it to around 3,000 acres, but after the Second World War, the 3rd Bt was created 1st Lord Sherwood in 1941 but sold the very large house to the newly created National Coal Board as offices in 1947. The house and almost 100 acres were sold to the Nottinghamshire County Council in 1973 and they promptly demolished both house and chapel to make way for a new police HQ.

74. Moira House, Arnold (II), 1978

Moira House was built in 1795 on land awarded to his family in the 1792 enclosure award by Gen. Sir Francis Rawdon (later Rawdon-Hastings), 2nd Earl of Moira, KG (1754–1826). He had inherited the estate, centered on Donington Hall, Leicestershire, through his wife, the heiress of the 10th Earl of Huntingdon, and which he offered to the exiled Bourbons during their exile. Indeed, the Dauphin (later Louis XVIII) is said to have been entertained at Moira House, which was intended purely as a hunting lodge. It was situated facing Front Street and was a relatively simple design of two piles of two and a half storeys (attic dormers on the garden front) with three bays, originally with tripartite windows flanking the entrance, but latterly these were replaced by square bays. The design was possibly provided by William Wilkins, whom Lord Moira had employed to rebuild Donington Hall. Moira was in 1816 created Marquess of Hastings, but on his death the house seems to have been detached from its estate and let. In 1853 the tenant was Wright Allen, a surgeon, but later most of the estates of the 4th Marquess had to be sold after he lost everything on the 1867 Derby. Allen's son, a GP, seems to have bought the freehold and was there until 1897. It was then acquired by Harvey Francis (who added the square bays to the façade and wide second-floor casements) and from 1926 by his son Dr John Francis. In 1965 it was bought by the Webber family who left around 1970 when it fell into dereliction, being demolished in 1978 to make way for a supermarket.

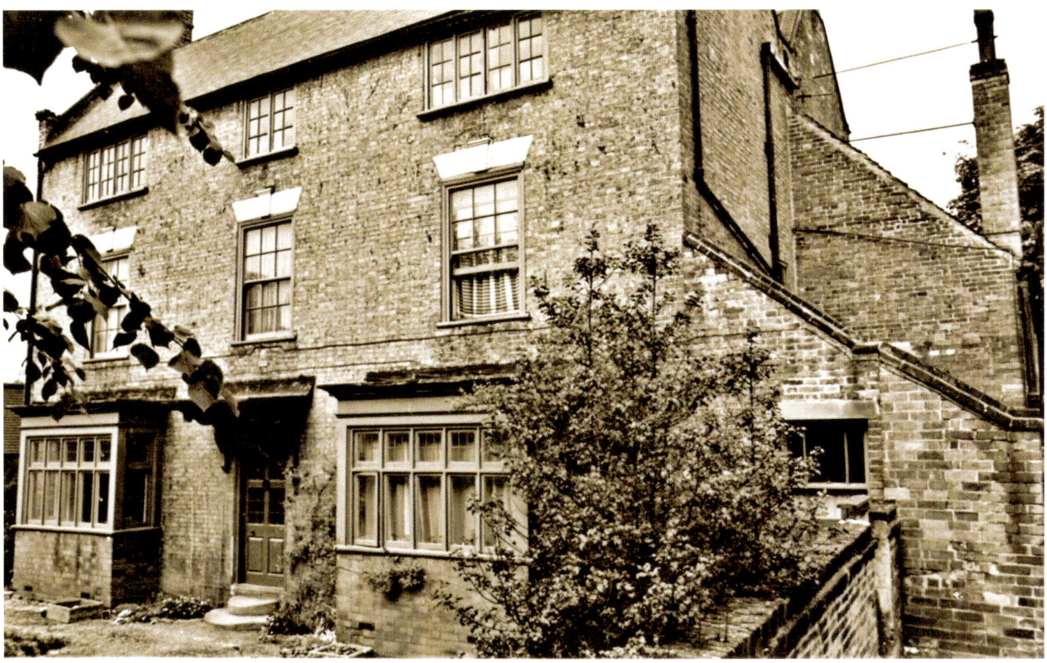

Moira House, 1976. (Bamfords Ltd)

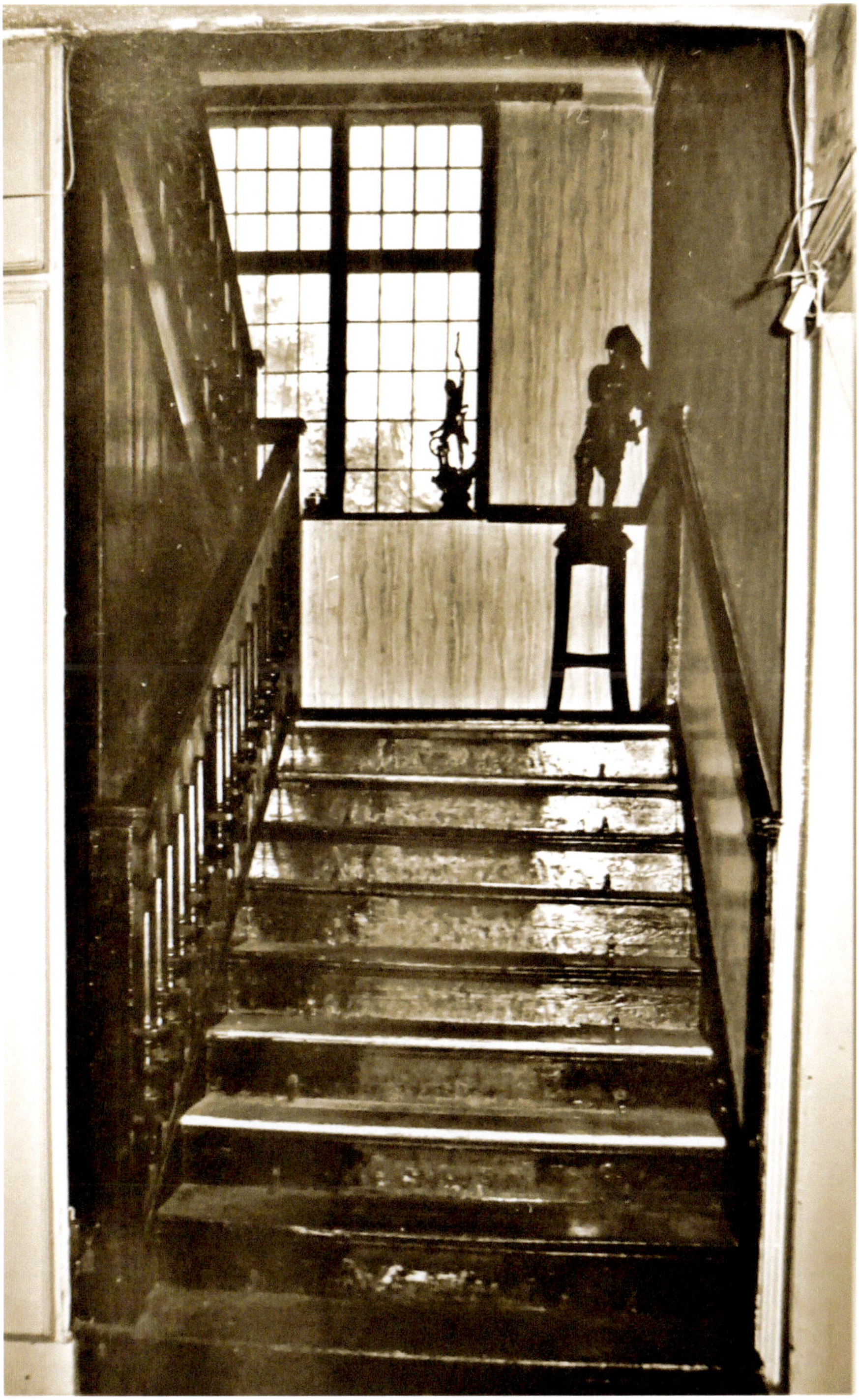

The main staircase of Moira House, 1976. (Bamfords Ltd)

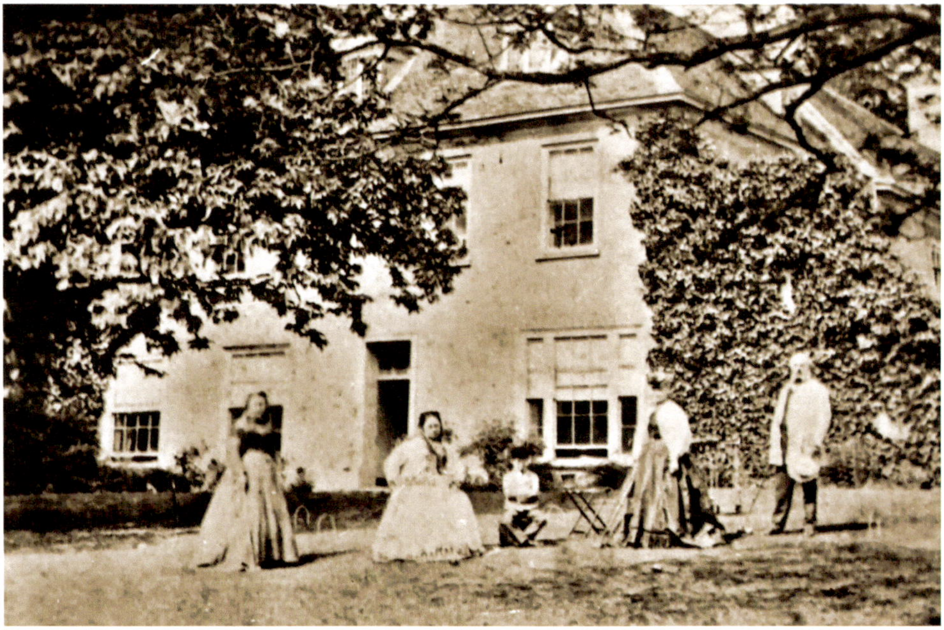

Moira House in 1865 with Dr Allen and family – before the addition of the square bays. (Bamfords Ltd)

75. Park Hall, Mansfield Woodhouse, by 1980

A late Tudor house existed here, the seat of the Digbys of Mansfield Woodhouse, who owned the estate until 1736 when it was sold to Lincolnshire landowner John Hall (1699–1763) who died there in 1763.It seems likely that the house was built before he married Mansfield Woodhouse co-heiress Mary Gould in 1764. It was essentially a pattern-book-style, two-and-a-half-storey Palladian villa with a Serlian window surmounted by a Thermal one over the entrance and flanked by a pair of full-height canted bays united by sill bands and illustrated as built on a Pinxton porcelain cup. One non-pattern book refinement inside was a circular cantilevered staircase with a wrought iron balustrade. Francis Hall JP DL (1805–88) extended the house in neo-Jacobean style, lower, of two storeys with attic gables, along with a grooved ashlar crenellated portico and he much improved the estate of 750 acres, but neither he nor his two successors produced any children. The last, Francis Hall KC (1856–1928), migrated to Canada with the contents, letting it to Sir John Houfton until 1926, when it was sold and he moved to Sherwood Hall (see p. 79) and Park Hall became a cyclists' hostel. It may have been Houfton who demolished all but one bay of the nineteenth-century wing and added matching classical ranges either side of the original house, suggesting the hand of his cousin Percy as architect. Quite why he needed to expand the house so much is unclear, and after the sale its size limited its reuse and, after the Second World War, it became empty, then derelict, the remains mainly being cleared away in the 1970s. The site is now covered with housing.

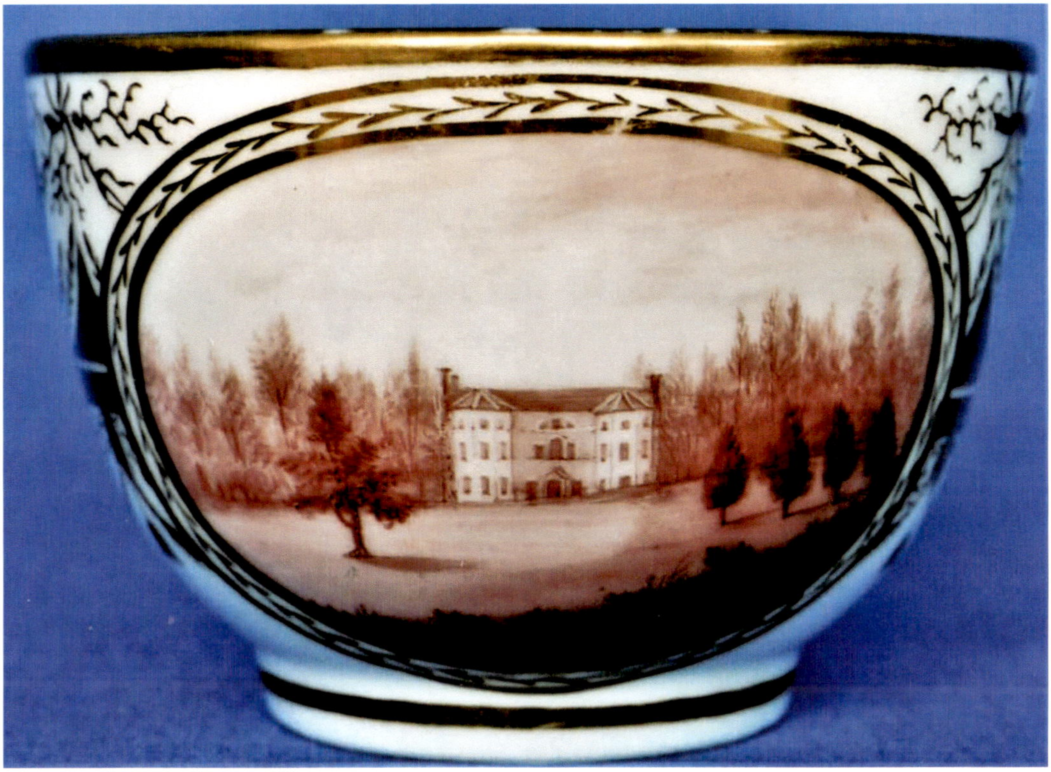

Park Hall painted as built onto an eighteenth-century Pinxton teacup. (Mellors & Kirk)

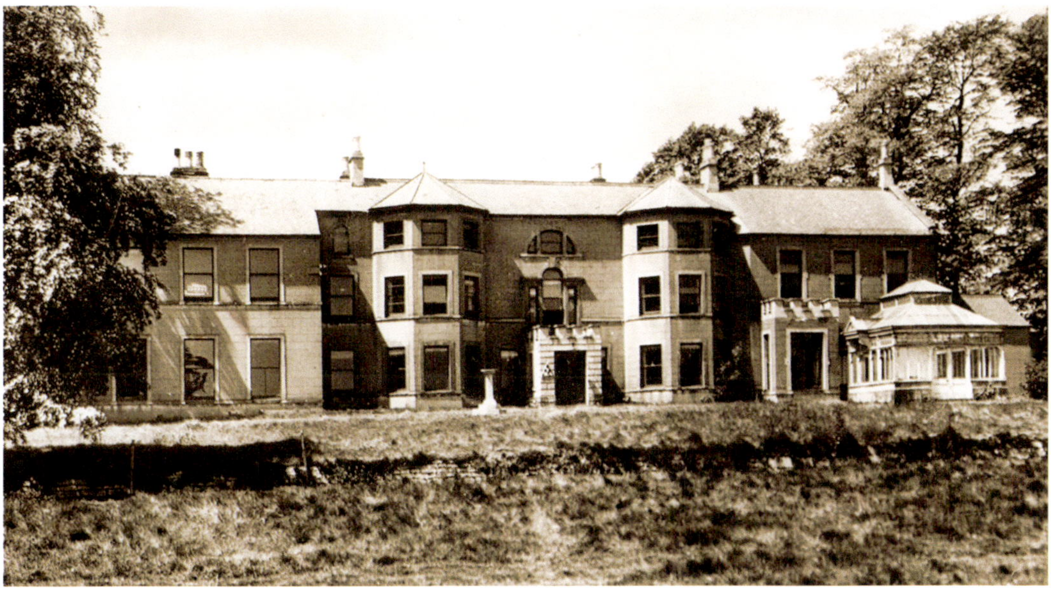

Park Hall as vastly extended. From a 1920s postcard. (James Darwin)

76. Lamcote House, Radcliffe on Trent, 1980

Long part of the Pierreponts' Holme estate, sometime before 1798 Nottingham confectioner John Topott JP DL (1749–1827) purchased a modest 25 acres at Radcliffe from Earl Manvers and built a modest brick two-storey villa, colloquially known as Sugar Plum Hall, possibly because of its colour-washed stucco. On Topott's death it came to his daughter, Henrietta Burnside, wife of the vicar of Plumtree, who let it first to banker and industrialist Francis Wright, later of Osmaston Manor, Derbyshire, then to lace manufacturer George Bacon and after him to Thomas Marriott JP (d. 1857). He was followed by Francis Wright's kinsman Ichabod Charles Wright (see Bramcote Hall, p. 84) to 1865. The house was then reoccupied by the Burnside family, who immediately set about rebuilding it, raising it by a storey with a bracketed cornice, modifying the fenestration (including plate glass windows), adding a substantial service wing and a rather heavy double-arched stone portico. The interior was refitted extensively and decorated with exotic timbers. Four Burnside sisters lived there until all but one married and moved away, along with their nephew, William Burnside, but in 1892 the youngest sister married (as his second wife) Hon. Henry Noel, a younger son of the 1st Earl of Gainsborough, and they moved in. She died a widow in 1904, whereupon the house was sold to Charles Birkin, CMG, TD, DL (1865–1932), younger son of lace making magnate Sir Thomas Birkin 1st Bt (born at Aspley Hall, see p. 85), whose daughter by his American wife was Freda Dudley Ward, later mistress of Edward VIII. From 1916 to 1919 the house became an auxiliary hospital. His son, later Sir Charles, 5th Bt, sold the house and 177 acres (essentially a single farm) to Sir Albert Ball who quickly sold on to Arthur Manchester, whose widow later converted the house into flats, all of which had become empty by 1980 and in July that year the house was demolished and the site redeveloped.

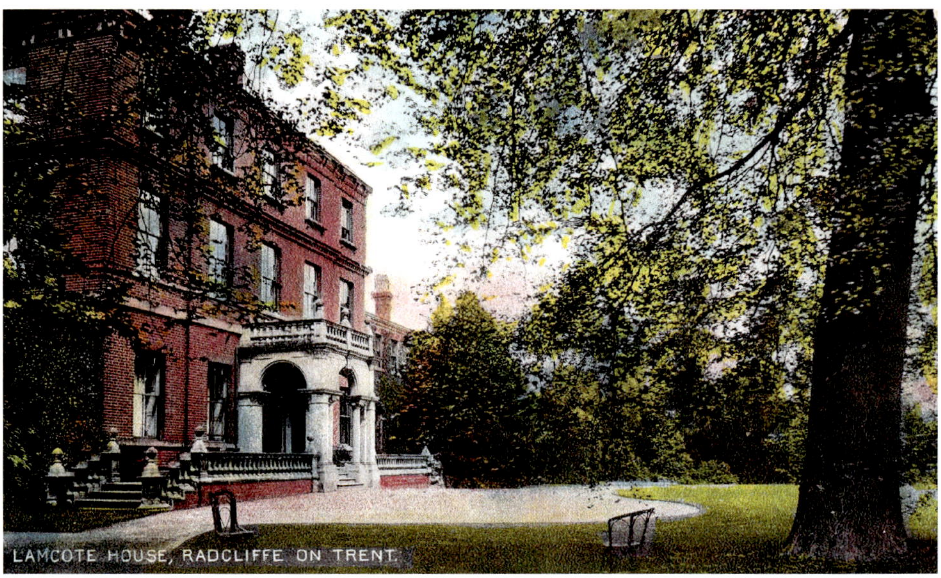

Lamcote House entrance front, *c.* 1900. From a chromolithographic postcard. (James Darwin)

Bibliography

Bonser, G. G., *A History of Sutton-in-Ashfield* (Sutton, 1949)

Brown, C., *A History of Nottinghamshire,* 2nd edition (London, 1896)

Cobbing, B. and Priestland, P., *Sir Thomas Stanhope of Shelford: Local Life in Elizabethan Times* (Radcliffe-on-Trent, 2003)

Girouard M. *Biographical. Dict. of English Architects 1540-1640* (New Haven & London, 2021)

Jacks, L., *The Great Houses of Nottinghamshire and the County Families* (Nottingham 1881)

Jones, P. E., *Lost Houses of Nottinghamshire* (Nottingham 2006)

Lindley, L., *History of Sutton-in-Ashfield or, Past Links with the Present* (Sutton 1907)

Mellors, R., *Old Nottingham Suburbs: Then and Now* (Nottingham 1914)

Pevsner, Sir N. and Williamson, E., *The Buildings of England: Nottinghamshire* (London, 1979)

Thoroton, J., ed., Throsby, J., *History and Antiquities of Nottinghamshire*, 3 Vols (London, 1792)

Thoroton Society, Transactions, *passim*.

Thorold, H., *A Shell Guide to Nottinghamshire* (London 1984)

Acknowledgements

The author stands in debt to a large number of people in the preparation of this book, not least those who helped so generously in various ways towards the various editions of the three editions of *The Derbyshire Country House,* and this publisher's *Lost Houses of Derbyshire*, to which my friend and former colleague Mick Stanley FGS contributed substantially; as a native of Mansfield Woodhouse, his services were called upon in researching this book too. To my wife Carole I owe immense thanks for her patience, support and her willingness to drive to outlying portions of Nottinghamshire for me, not to mention taking occasional photographs. Nor can one omit the kindness of Amberley Publishing and the helpfulness of Nick Grant in particular, constrained as they were by Covid-19, still (it is to be hoped) in its death throes as this book was prepared for publication. My friend James Darwin, chief case worker of the Georgian Group and a former colleague, has been extremely helpful in numerous ways and had also kindly supplied copies of photographs, mainly postcards, of houses absent from my own collection.

The resources of Nottinghamshire Record Office, the University of Nottingham Library and help of English Heritage/Historic England and a variety of local history and civic societies have been invaluable, not to mention the wealth of knowledge published in the august pages of the Transactions of the Thoroton Society.

Heartfelt thanks are also due to David Coke-Steel, the late Sir Howard Colvin, the late Don Farnsworth, Sir Richard FitzHerbert, Bt, the late B. F. J. Pardoe, the late Edward Saunders, Robert Innes-Smith and many others, without whom this book would not have been remotely possible. Others who have kindly made illustrations available are acknowledged with the relevant picture, although some have chosen to remain anonymous. Every effort has been made to identify and contact the correct originators of photographs; where I have failed, the presence of the images testify to my gratitude.

The author would also be most pleased to hear, too, from anyone who can throw further light upon any of the houses mentioned, or others omitted (this mainly due to the paucity of illustrations) or are able to offer corrections, for any mistakes are entirely my own, and in a work of this scope, impossible wholly to avoid.